MIDLANDS SOCCER AT WAR

by
Tony Matthews

Acknowledgments

I would like to thank the following people who have helped me with the compilation, preparation and publication of this book: The staff of Windmill Print & Design (Cradley Heath), namely Dave Dain, Sheila Dudley, Derek Gardner, Phil Shakespeare, Lee Shaw, Doug Vallender and Patrick Shread; fellow statisticians Dr. Geoff Allman, Martin O'Connor, Jack Rollin and Gordon Andrews; Sporting Pictures (U.K.) and the Express & Star Picture Library (Wolverhampton); Mrs Christine Povey, and last but not least my wife Margaret who once again slaved hard and long proof-reading the manuscript.

Contents

FIRST PUBLISHED in Great Britain by
SPORTS LEISURE CONCEPTS,
Portersfield Road,
Cradley Heath,
Warley,
West Midlands.
B64 7BX

ISBN 1 873171 01 3

Printed by WINDMILL PRINT & DESIGN
Portersfield Road, Cradley Heath,
Warley, West Midlands. B64 7BX
(Telephone: 0384 60171)

Introduction

In early August 1939, when the players dutifully reported back to their respective clubs for pre-season training, the atmosphere was one of apprehension and uncertainty.

Banner headlines of various newspapers clearly predicted 'Football to go if war comes.'

On 21st August, the F.A. decided to forego Rule 33 which stated that 'no player serving in His Majesty's Forces could be registered as a professional footballer.' And when the opening day fixtures got underway five days later, over 600,000 spectators attended the 44 matches, with 120,000 witnessing games involving the six Midland clubs, Villa, Birmingham, Coventry, Walsall, West Bromwich Albion and Wolves. Wolves, in fact, pulled in a 41,222 gate for the visit of Arsenal to Molineux.

Following the normal series of midweek matches, Friday 1st September saw the start of the evacuation of children from London, but it was agreed that the scheduled Saturday afternoon fixtures should go ahead as planned — and they did. On the same day the Germans invaded Poland but no matches were cancelled although in the capital, Arsenal's home game with Sunderland and Fulham's with Luton Town were both delayed with kick-off times being put back to 5.00pm and 6.00pm respectively because of the strong possibility that the traffic could be seriously disrupted by the evacuation scheme. With people's minds obviously concentrated on other things, it was no surprise that the overall attendance figure shrunk to 380,000.

There were hold-ups all over the country — and Tottenham arrived at The Hawthorns for their Second Division game with West Bromwich Albion just two minutes before the scheduled kick-off time. At Blackpool, a bottle was tossed on to the pitch close to the Wolves' goalkeeper Alex Scott, and the referee instructed that two constables should patrol behind the visitors' goal throughout the game.

On the morning of Sunday 3rd September, it was universally declared that 'Britain was at War' and competitive Football came to a halt — for the time being. There was an immediate ban on the assembly of crowds until further notice but 48 hours later the Football League President, Mr. W.C. Cuff, announced publicly that all clubs should retain their players under contract to stand by, as a result of the Government's order to close all places of entertainment.

These seven points effectively ended League action in September 1939:

1. The advice to the clubs to keep players standing by was cancelled and the clubs were liable to pay players up to September 6.
2. Signing-on bonuses and removal expenses were to be cleared immediately.
3. Season ticket refunds could not yet be given but must be made uniform.
4. Those matches already played in the League were to be counted as cup-ties and if the regular schedule resumed later the return matches would be played on similar terms.
5. Injured players were to follow end-of-season procedures when making claims.
6. Proposed Inter-League games with Scotland and Ireland were cancelled.
7. Any alternate schemes for competition when soccer resumed were deferred.

The general flow of organised League and Cup football in Britain was seriously disrupted by World War Two — and several players up and down the country had their respective careers virtually ruined due to the hostilities which took place in Europe between 1939 and 1945.

After just three matches had been fulfilled at the start of the 1939-40 season, League Football was abandoned, yet following a relatively shortish interlude, competitive games recommenced and all but Aston Villa of the six West Midlands clubs, entered the systematically developed Regional Leagues for the remainder of that ill-fated campaign.

In fact, during the previous 1938-39 season, quite a few footballers had joined the Territorial Army or other National Service Organisations, and they indeed, spent their leisure time preparing for the seemingly inevitable conflict which arose in September 1939!

In April 1939, the F.A. issued a circular encouraging players to display a patriotic example to the youth of the nation!

Several opted for the Terriers and Militia, while others preferred to wear totally different uniforms.

Consequently, as more reservists were called up, it was duly recorded at the Football League Management Committee meeting in July of that year, that 'there is no onus on clubs to pay players called up for military service during their period of military training.

'If, however, arrangements can be made with the Military Authorities for the players' services on match days, their liability would arise during such week (or weeks) as the players are available for the club.'

Hardly any reference at all was made to war at the A.G.M. of the Association and League in the summer of 1939.

There were, however, certain decisions made concerning the domestic soccer scene, and these included Walsall (who received 35 votes) being re-elected to the Third Division (South).

The watering of pitches before November and after February was officially sanctioned (and Wolves were delighted), and also, by a majority of 24 to 20, it was agreed for the first time that all players must wear numbered shirts in League matches.

In the popular 'News Chronicle Football Annual' of 1939-40, Charlie Buchan, the former Sunderland, Arsenal and England forward, referred to the last full peacetime campaign before World War Two as being 'an eventful season that proceeded merrily despite alarms of war and cries in world affairs.'

Four players were recognised as being outstanding during 1938-39, among them Bill Morris, the Wolves full-back, who went on to serve the Molineux club splendidly during the hostilities.

After a period of serious discussions, it was finally agreed that football should recommence with clubs playing in Regional Sections up and down the country. And on 21st October 1939 soccer was again a sporting pastime, with players certainly enjoying themselves out on the park as these results clearly indicated: Arsenal 8 Charlton 4; West Ham 2 Crystal Palace 6; Leicester 6 Walsall 1; Chesterfield 8 Lincoln 0; Port Vale 6 Crewe Alexandra 1; Everton 4 Stoke City 4; Wrexham 6 New Brighton 4 and Manchester United 0 Manchester City 4.

When things were finally sorted out, five of the Midland clubs (with the exception of Aston Villa who decided to play in the local Birmingham & District League) were placed in the Regional League, Midland Division, along with Luton, Northampton and Leicester City.

In the interests of public safety, there was a limit put on attendances. This was set initially at 8,000 or half the capacity of the ground, whichever the less, in evacuation areas or as fixed by the local Police.

For grounds situated in other areas which had an extra-large capacity of 60,000 or more, the Chief Constable had discretion to allow crowds of up to 15,000 — as long as the matches in question were made 'all ticket' and that tickets be purchased in advance!

The Football League also sanctioned a payment of 30 shillings (£1.50) per match to each player for seasons 1939-40 to 1942-43 inclusive. In 1943-44 this amount was increased to £2.00 a man and by 1945-46 it had been upped to £4.00.

Competition throughout the duration of the war was excellent — and very well supported. There were plenty of entertaining matches and gradually the crowds increased. Players guested for many different clubs, and most of them served in the Forces at one time or another.

Taking each Midland club in turn, ASTON VILLA did not play any major football (in the Regional League) for three seasons, choosing instead to fulfil fixtures in the local Birmingham & District League, taking part in various Midland Cup competitions. In fact, they did not use Villa Park for some considerable time, playing their home matches instead at Solihull Town's ground. Villa Park, in the meantime, was given over to war use. The Trinity Road stand was converted into an air-raid shelter and ammunition stores; the home dressing

Aston Villa, winners of the Football League (North) Cup in 1944:
Back row (left to right): Mr. Phil Hunt (trainer), Ronnie Starling, Mr Joe Broughton (director), Mr Fred Normansell (Chairman), Mr Chris Buckley (director), Ernie Callaghan, Alan Wakeman.
Middle row: Mr Norman Smith (director), Bob Iverson, Alex Massie, George Cummings, Harry Parkes, Mr Edward Smith (director).
Front row: George Edwards, Vic Potts, Frank Broome and Eric Houghton.

room was utilised by the Rifle Company of the 9th Royal Warwickshire Regiment and other offices were put into practical use offering facilities for staff of the Police Force, Fire Brigade and First Aid divisions.

Work was allowed to continue on the extension of the Holte End terracing (completed by February 1940) although it was, of course, to stand empty until Villa resumed playing 'at home' in season 1942-43.

In 1942-43 Villa entered the Football League (North) and reached the semi-final of the wartime Cup, losing to Blackpool on aggregate. But revenge was gained over the 'Seasiders' the following season when the 'claret and blues' pulled off a memorable victory by beating Blackpool over two legs to take the trophy away from Bloomfield Road.

In 1945 Villa reached the Midland Wartime Cup Final only to lose 9-0 on aggregate to Derby County.

The 1945-46 campaign saw the return of a 42-match League programme and Villa finished second to neighbours Birmingham City in the 'South' championship, losing out on goal-average, despite scoring 106 goals, 39 of which came from the boot of George Edwards.

BIRMINGHAM, who added the name City to their title in the summer of 1945, unlike Villa, played in the Midland Regional League in 1939-40 and finished a creditable third in the final table despite having to play all their games away from St. Andrews from October to March, when the ground was closed because of the threat of air-raids on the city.

These were difficult times for Birmingham — and travelling home from an away match at Luton, the team coach crashed through a traffic island during the 'black out' but thankfully no one on board was injured.

Walsall provided the opposition to Blues when St. Andrews 're-opened' on 23rd March 1940 and a crowd of 12,000 saw the Saddlers beaten 2-1.

At the end of this season Harry Hibbs said farewell to football, and of course to Birmingham. He announced his retirement and a Benefit Match was staged at St. Andrews in his honour, Birmingham beating Aston Villa 2-1 infront of 15,000 spectators.

In 1940-41 Blues took part in the League South but were only able to play 16 matches — this being due to severe bomb damage at St. Andrews. The 1941 summer saw further enemy action on the ground and the club was asked to stage competitive games there only at the beginning of the season and again at the end, when the weather would be at its best. This, however, did not materialise and in the end Blues played only friendly matches until resuming in the League North in August 1942.

During this season ('42-43) they played all their home games at Villa Park and it wasn't until August 1943 that they were able to return to St. Andrews, which had suffered another blow in January 1942 when the main stand was burnt down following an incident whereby a fireman threw a bucket of petrol over a brazier thinking he was drenching it with water!

Repair work was carried out at regular intervals at St. Andrews and it was not finally completed until 1946-47.

The team, meanwhile 'soldiered' on and in 1945-46 they almost achieved the 'double' winning the League South title (from rivals Villa) and losing to Derby County after a replay in the semi-final of the F.A. Cup. Over 145,000 fans witnessed the two clashes against County — 65,013 at Hillsborough and a massive 80,480 at Maine Road — this being the biggest crowd to assemble during the wartime period to watch two club sides.

Harry Storer had been appointed manager at St. Andrews in June 1945, leaving Coventry City to take over the Blues — and he did an excellent job in his first season with his new club.

Storer's former club COVENTRY CITY started off their wartime exploits playing in the Regional League Midland Division — and they finished in 4th place at the end of the 1939-40 season.

Unfortunately after having got through just ten games of the following season's League South programme Coventry's ground at Highfield Road was severely damaged by enemy bombs and consequently no more fixtures were undertaken until the start of the 1942-43 campaign when they entered the League North competition. They used 50 players this season, including a handful of guests, among them Gil Merrick (Blues).

Coventry's worst wartime season — in terms of results — came in 1944-45. They played 39 matches and won only 12, losing 19 and conceding 94 goals.

There followed a mediocre campaign in the Football League South of 1945-46 when 13th position was attained. Harry Barratt top-scored with a total of 27 goals in League and Cup — and among the 41 players used this term, two were 'foreigners' (Bilbao and Aldecoa), Fred Gardner was the Warwickshire cricketer and Eric Houghton guested from Aston Villa.

WALSALL participated in each of the seven wartime seasons. They fulfilled a total of 245 matches and were undefeated in 134 of them, scoring over 450 goals. Unfortunately they finished bottom of the Midlands Regional League in 1939-40, picking up just 19 points out of a possible 56.

There followed a mediocre campaign in the Football League South of 1945-46 when 13th position was attained. Harry Barratt top-scored with a total of 27 goals in League and Cup — and among the 41 players used this term, two were 'foreigners' (Bilbao and Aldecoa), Fred Gardner was the Warwickshire cricketer and Eric Houghton guested from Aston Villa.

WALSALL participated in each of the seven wartime seasons. They fulfilled a total of 245 matches and were undefeated in 134 of them, scoring over 450 goals. Unfortunately they finished bottom of the Midlands Regional League in 1939-40, picking up just 19 points out of a possible 56.

In 1940-41 they ended up higher than Albion, Birmingham, Leicester, Northampton, Stoke, Nottingham Forest and Notts County in the League South, with only Coventry City doing better in the table, although the Highfield Road club only played 10 games. Walsall, in fact, claimed over 100 goals this season and were beaten by Leicester (2-0) in the Midland Cup Final.

Nothing outstanding was achieved in 1941-42 or in 1942-43. Indeed, in the latter season Walsall struggled in the second phase of the League North competition and eventually finished third from bottom (with 8 points out of 32).

In 1943-44 they faired no better dropping down a place in the final table of the League North championship — Walsall having the same points total (12) as Tranmere (the bottom club) and Wolves, who finished a place above them. There came another frustrating season in 1944-45, Walsall taking nothing out of the League or Cup competitions and having to settle for a position third off the bottom in the final table (Second Championship).

But then, in the transitional season of 1945-46, the Saddlers' faithful at last got something to cheer when Walsall reached the final of the League South Cup, only to lose 1-0 to Bournemouth.

WEST BROMWICH ALBION did not enjoy a great deal of success either during the 1939-46 period.

They collected only one honour — taking the Midland Cup (at Nottingham Forest's expense) in season 1943-44, winning the two-legged final in 'extra — extra-time' 6-5 on aggregate.

In the Midland Division in 1939-40 the Baggies finished second in the table behind Wolves (41 points to 40); in 1940-41 they had to settle for a mid-table slot in the League South championship but missed glory the following season when the 'League' organising the final positions on average points, gained from 18 matches, dropped Albion into second place, 0.1 of a point behind Leicester City, the declared champions. Leicester, in fact, ended up with 25 points from 17 games for an average of 26.40, while Albion achieved 19 points out of 13 matches for an average of 26.30.

There was nothing to shout about in 1942-43, or indeed, after that success (in the Midland Cup) of 1944. Albion in fact just squeezed into the North Cup competition in 1944-45 (on goal-average from Blackburn) yet their form overall was disappointing. They did better in 1945-46 finishing fifth in the League South table, nine points behind the champions Birmingham.

WOLVES, under the guidance initially of Major Frank Buckley and then managed by Ted Vizard, had several ups and downs during the war.

They played a total of 233 competitive matches (255 all told including friendlies) and they won a couple of prizes — the Midland Regional League Championship in 1939-40 and the Wartime League (North) Cup in 1941-42, when they beat Sunderland over two legs in a pulsating final which attracted a combined attendance figure of almost 78,000.

Wolves, in fact, did not field a team during the 1940-41 season — and most of their players drifted away to 'guest' for other clubs, Messrs. Wright and Mullen choosing Leicester City, and these two future England internationals helped themselves to winners medals when the 'Filberts' beat Walsall 2-0 to carry off the Midland Cup.

In the first season of the war, Wolves lost almost £18,000 and the following season (when they never kicked a ball in earnest) the club lost well over £4,500.

During the 1939-46 period Wolves had some famous players in their side (as guests) and these included the likes of Jack Rowley (Manchester United) who scored eight goals against Derby County in one match — to set a record for marksmanship by an individual player at Molineux.

Birmingham City, pictured in 1945.
Back row (left to right): Sid Owen, Ted Duckhouse, Gil Merrick, Dave Massart, Fred Harris.
Front row: "Jock" Mulraney, "Neil" Dougall, Dennis Jennings, Arthur Turner, Harold Bodle and George Edwards.

International Section
(Midlands' International Matches)

There were four major international matches played in the Midlands during the war — and these were staged at four different venues, the details of which are as follows:-

25th October 1941 — At St. Andrews (Birmingham)
ENGLAND 2 WALES 1 (Half time 2-0)

England: Marks (Arsenal); Bacuzzi (Fulham), Hapgood (Arsenal); Goslin (Bolton Wanderers), Cullis (Wolves), Mercer (Everton); Matthews (Stoke City), Edelston (Reading), Welsh (Charlton Athletic), Hagan (Sheffield United), D. Compton (Arsenal).

Wales: Poland (Liverpool); Turner (Charlton Athletic), Hughes (Birmingham); Green (Charlton Athletic), T.G. Jones (Everton), Witcomb (W.B.A.); Hopkins (Brentford), James (Cardiff City), Dearson (Birmingham), L. Jones (Arsenal), Cumner (Arsenal).

Scorers: England — Hagan, Edelston. Wales — Hopkins.

Attendance: 24,831

24th October 1942 — At Molineux (Wolverhampton)
ENGLAND 1 WALES 2 (Half time 1-1)

England: Marks (Arsenal); Hardwick (Middlesbrough), Hapgood (Arsenal); Britton (Everton), Cullis (Wolves), Mercer (Everton); Matthews (Stoke City), Rooke (Fulham), Lawton (Everton), Gibbons (Tottenham Hotspur), Mullen (Wolves).

Wales: Poland (Liverpool); Turner (Charlton Athletic), Hughes (Birmingham); Dearson (Birmingham), T.G. Jones (Everton), Powell (Q.P.R.); Hopkins (Brentford), Lucas (Swindon Town), Lowrie (Coventry City), B. Jones (Arsenal), Cumner (Arsenal).

Scorers: England — Lawton. Wales — Cumner 2.

Attendance: 25,097.

3rd February 1945 — At Villa Park (Birmingham)
ENGLAND 3 SCOTLAND 2 (Half time 1-1)

England: Swift (Manchester City); Scott (Arsenal), Hardwick (Middlesbrough); Soo (Stoke City), Franklin (Stoke City), Mercer (Everton); Matthews (Stoke City), R. Brown (Charlton Athletic), Lawton (Everton), Mortensen (Blackpool), Smith (Brentford).

Scotland: Brown (Queen's Park); Harley (Liverpool), Stephen (Bradford); Busby (Liverpool), Thyne (Darlington), Macauley (West Ham United); Delaney (Celtic), Fagan (Liverpool), Dodds (Blackpool), Black (Hearts), Liddell (Liverpool).

Scorers: England — Mortensen 2, R. Brown.
Scotland — Delaney, Dodds.

Attendance: 65,780.

20th October 1945 — At The Hawthorns (West Bromwich)
ENGLAND 0 WALES 1 (Half time 0-1)

England: Williams (Wolves); Scott (Arsenal), Kinsell (W.B.A.); Soo (Leicester City), Franklin (Stoke City), Mercer (Everton); Matthews (Stoke City), Fenton (Middlesbrough), Stubbins (Newcastle United), Barrass (Bolton Wanderers), Watson (Huddersfield Town).

Wales: Sidlow (Wolves); Winter (Bolton Wanderers), Hughes (Birmingham); Dearson (Birmingham), Davies (Nottingham Forest), Burgess (Tottenham Hotspur); Powell (Leeds United), Astbury (Chester), Lowrie (Coventry City), Lucas (Swindon Town), Edwards (Birmingham).

* Kinsell (England) and Lowrie (Wales) were both sent-off for fighting. The gate receipts of £8,573 created a new record for The Hawthorns.

Scorer: Wales — Powell.

Attendance: 54,611.

Wolves and Wales goalkeeper Cyril Sidlow (centre) and Don Dearson of Birmingham (No4) thwart an England attack in the International Match at The Hawthorns in October 1945.

Other Representative Matches played in the Midlands: 1939-46

(not including games against League clubs)

26th December 1939 — At Molineux
FOOTBALL LEAGUE XI 3 ALL BRITISH XI 3

Football League XI: Scott (Wolves); Hayes (Huddersfield), Hapgood (Arsenal); Gardner (Burnley), Cullis (Wolves), Mercer (Everton); Matthews (Stoke), Martin (Aston Villa), Lawton (Everton), Butt (Blackburn), Bastin (Arsenal).

British XI: Riley (Barnsley); Cook (Everton), Cummings (Aston Villa); Dearson (Birmingham), Harper (Barnsley), McNab (W.B.A.); Broome (Aston Villa), Mutch (P.N.E.), Dodds (Blackpool), Doherty (Manchester City), Beasley (Huddersfield).

Scorers: Football League XI — Butt 2, Lawton.
British XI — Beasley 2, Doherty.

Attendance: 18,000.

28th February 1942 — At Molineux
RAF (AMATEURS) 6 BELGIUM ARMY 3

RAF: Williams (Walsall); Whittaker, Sergeant; Leek, Joy (Arsenal), Wright; Acquaroff (Norwich City), Anderson, Gibbons (Tottenham), Riley, L.C. Finch (Barnet).

Scorers: RAF — Gibbons 4, Acquaroff, Finch.

Attendance: 2,142.

2nd May 1942 — At Molineux
FOOTBALL LEAGUE 5 WESTERN COMMAND 2

Football League: Scott (Wolves); Brigham (Stoke), A.J. Smith (Chelsea); Shankly (P.N.E.), Morgan (Walsall), Haycock (Aston Villa); Matthews (Stoke), Fagan (Liverpool), Dodds (Blackpool), Dearson (Birmingham), Liddell (Liverpool).

Western Command: Hamilton (Queen's Park); Reid (Kilmarnock), Cumberbridge (Stoke); Chilton (Manchester United), Pryde (Blackburn), Angus (Exeter); Hamilton (Newcastle), Balmer (Liverpool), Robinson (Wolves), Dix (Tottenham), Armes (Middlesbrough).

Scorers: Football League — Dodds 3, Fagan, Dearson.
Western Command — Robinson 2, Balmer.

Attendance: 5,443.

12th February 1944 — At Molineux
WESTERN COMMAND 3 R.A.F. (NW) 5

Western Command: Swift (Manchester City); Sproston (Manchester City), Kinsell (WBA); Moore (Grimsby), Pryde (Blackburn), Taylor (Bolton); Elliott (W.B.A.), Lucas (Swindon), Lawton (Everton), Black (Hearts), Duns (Sunderland).

R.A.F.: Savage (Manchester United); Pope (Blackpool), Clarke (Manchester City); Bray (Manchester City), Hayward (Blackpool), Slack (Norwich); Matthews (Stoke), Carter (Sunderland), Mortensen (Blackpool), Doherty (Manchester City), Pearson (Newcastle).

Scorers: Western Command — Lawton 2, Pryde.
R.A.F. — Carter 2, Doherty 2, Mortensen.

Attendance: 22,906.

20th January 1945 — At Highfield Road (Coventry)
F.A. XI 4 R.A.F. 6

F.A. XI: Merrick (Birmingham); Sproston (Manchester City), Kinsell (W.B.A.); Franklin (Stoke), G. Smith (Charlton), Mercer (Everton); Broome (Aston Villa), Shackleton (Bradford P.A.), Lawton (Everton), Edelston (Reading), Burbanks (Sunderland).

R.A.F.: Williams (Walsall); Scott (Arsenal), Hardwick (Middlesbrough); Soo (Stoke), A. Brown (Huddersfield), Layton (Reading); L. Smith (Brentford), R. Brown (Charlton), Dodds (Blackpool), Mortensen (Blackpool), Pearson (Newcastle).

Scorers: F.A. XI — Shackleton 2, Franklin, Lawton.
R.A.F. — Mortensen 3, Dodds 2, L. Smith.

Attendance: 12,750.

24th February 1945 — At Molineux
WESTERN COMMAND 2 NORTHERN COMMAND 0

Western Command: Swift (Manchester City); Sproston (Manchester City), Jefferson (Q.P.R.); Wright (Wolves), Tudor (W.B.A.), Welsh (Charlton); Chapman (Oldham), Lucas (Swindon), Lawton (Everton), Black (Hearts). Watson (Huddersfield).

Northern Command: Sidlow (Wolves); Gadsby (Leeds), Nicholson (Tottenham); Heyden (Derby County), Blenkinsopp (Grimsby), Wharton (Portsmouth); Hunt (Sheffield Wednesday), Hold (Bradford City), Dewis (Leicester), Gordon (Newcastle), Mullen (Wolves).

Scorers: Western Command — Lucas, Lawton.

Attendance: 16,148

PRICE ONE PENNY
THE WOLVES
Official Programme
Saturday, Feb. 28th, 1942. Kick-off 3-0 p.m.
INTER-ALLIED SERVICES CUP COMPETITION (Round 1)
NAMES AND POSITIONS OF PLAYERS.
BELGIAN ARMY IN GREAT BRITAIN
Colours - Shirts, Red. Knickers, Black.
RIGHT LEFT
A. CRICKELIE (2) M. HUWAERT (1)
A. WILLEMS (4) R. BILLET (5) C. LEGRAND (3)
M. KENENS (7) E. DE BUSSER (8) A. LANDRIEU (9) J. SCHUERMANS (10) G. VAN DEN BOSSCH (6) A. CLERINCKX (11)
Referee— W. H. CLINTON (Wolverhampton)
Linesmen— Red Stripe P. Vrydag (Belgian Army) Blue Stripe F/Lt. J. B. Birkhead, R.A.F.
F/LT. F. RILEY (10) (England & Corinthians)
F/SGT. L. C. FINCH (11) (England & Barnet.)
F/SGT. A. H. GIBBONS (9) (England & Spurs.)
SGT. R. S. ANDERSON (8) (England & Dulwich)
A.C. R. E. WRIGHT (6) (England & Walthamstow)
P/O B JOY (5) (England & Arsenal)
SGT. G. COLLINS (7) (R.A.F.)
SGT. G. SERGEANT (3) (F.A. XI & Romford)
CPL. T. H. LEEK (4) (England & Moor Green)
SGT. W. WHITTAKER (2) (England & Kingstonian)
SGT. B. F. WILLIAMS (1) (Walsall)
LEFT RIGHT
R.A.F. AMATEUR XI
Colours—Shirts, Blue Knickers, Dark.
THE TEAMS ARE SUBJECT TO ALTERATION

Gil Merrick

International Honours

The following players appeared for their country at International level during the wartime period:

1939-40

England

F. Broome (Aston Villa) v Scotland — May 1940
S. Cullis (Wolves) v Wales — November 1939
v Wales — April 1940
v Scotland — May 1940
J. Martin (Aston Villa) v Wales — Nov. 1939 (1 goal)
v Scotland — May 1940
D. Westcott (Wolves) v Wales — April 1940

Wales

D. Dearson (Birmingham) v England — November 1939
v England — April 1940
W. Hughes (Birmingham) v England — November 1939
C. Sidlow (Wolves) v England — November 1939
v England — April 1940
D. Witcomb (W.B.A.) v England — November 1939
v England — April 1940

1940-41

England

S. Cullis (Wolves) v Scotland — February 1941
v Wales — April 1941
v Scotland — May 1941
v Wales — June 1941

Wales

D. Dearson (Birmingham) v England — April 1941
v England — June 1941
W. Hughes (Birmingham) v England — April 1941
v England — June 1941
C. Sidlow (Wolves) v England — April 1941
v England — June 1941
D. Witcomb (W.B.A.) v England — Apr 1941 (1 goal)
v England — June 1941

1941-42

England

S. Cullis (Wolves) v Scotland — October 1941
v Wales — October 1941
v Scotland — June 1942
G. Mason (Coventry) v Scotland — April 1942
v Wales — May 1942

Wales

D. Dearson (Birmingham) v England — October 1941
v England — May 1942
W. Hughes (Birmingham) v England — October 1941
v England — May 1942
G. Lowrie (Coventry) v England — May 1942
D. Witcomb (W.B.A.) v England — October 1941
v England — May 1942

1942-43

England

S. Cullis (Wolves) v Scotland — October 1942
v Wales — October 1942
v Wales — February 1943
v Scotland — April 1943
v Wales — May 1943
J. Mullen (Wolves) v Wales — October 1942
D. Westcott (Wolves) v Wales — Feb 1943 (3 goals)
v Scotland —April 1943 (1 goal)
v Wales — May 1943 (1 goal)

Wales

D. Dearson (Birmingham) v England — October 1942
v England — February 1943
v England — May 1943
W. Hughes (Birmingham) v England — October 1942
v England — February 1943
v England — May 1943
G. Lowrie (Coventry) v England — October 1942
v England — Feb 1943 (3 goals)
v England — May 1943 (1 goal)
C. Sidlow (Wolves) v England — May 1943

1943-44

England

S. Cullis (Wolves) v Wales — September 1943
v Scotland — October 1943
v Scotland — February 1944
v Scotland — April 1944
v Wales — May 1944
W. Elliott (W.B.A.) v Wales — May 1944
F. Taylor (Wolves) v Scotland — April 1944

Wales

D. Dearson (Birmingham) v England — September 1943
v England — May 1944
W. Hughes (Birmingham) v England — September 1943
G. Lowrie (Coventry) v England — Sept 1943 (2 goals)
v England — May 1944
S. Morris (Birmingham) v England — May 1944
C. Sidlow (Wolves) v England — September 1943
v England — May 1944

1944-45

England

J. Mullen (Wolves) v Wales — September 1944
B. Williams (Walsall) v Wales — May 1945
v France — May 1945

Wales

D. Dearson (Birmingham) v England — Sept 1944 (1 goal)
v England — May 1945
G. Edwards (Coventry C) v England — May 1945 (1 goal)
W. Hughes (Birmingham) v England — September 1944
v England — May 1945
G. Lowrie (Coventry) v England — September 1944
C. Sidlow (Wolves) v England — September 1944
v England — May 1945

Scotland

G. Cummings (Aston Villa) v England — October 1944
J. Harris (Wolves) v England — April 1945

1945-46

England

W. Elliott (W.B.A.) v Scotland — April 1946
H. Kinsell (W.B.A.) v Ireland — September 1945
v Wales — October 1945
J. Mullen (Wolves) v Belgium — January 1946
L. Smith (Aston Villa) v France — May 1946
B. Williams (Wolves) v Wales — October 1945
v France — May 1946
W. Wright (Wolves) v Belgium — January 1946
v Scotland — April 1946
v Switzerland — May 1946
v France — May 1946

Scotland

N. Dougall (Birmingham) v England — April 1946

Wales

D. Dearson (Birmingham) v England — October 1945
v Scotland — November 1945
G. Edwards (Birmingham) v England — October 1945
v Scotland — November 1945
W. Hughes (Birmingham) v England — October 1945
v Scotland — November 1945
v Ireland — May 1946
G. Lowrie (Coventry) v England — October 1945
v Scotland — November 1945
C. Sidlow (Wolves) v England — October 1945
v Scotland — November 1945
D. Witcomb (W.B.A.) v Scotland — November 1945

Wartime International Appearances

Stan Cullis 20 for England
Don Dearson 15 for Wales
Billy Hughes 14 for Wales
Cyril Sidlow 11 for Wales

Picture Parade

Billy Elliott, Albion's flying winger and the Midlands top scorer during the war with 117 goals.

Wolves' England international trio of Jimmy Mullen (top), Billy Wright and Bert Williams.

George Cummings (Aston Villa and Scotland)

Don Dearson (Birmingham and Wales)

George Lowrie (Coventry City and Wales)

Wartime Representative Honours

1939-40
F.A. XI: F. Broome (Aston Villa), J. Martin (Aston Villa).
Football League XI: S. Cullis (Wolves, 2 apps), G. Cummings (Aston Villa), A. McNab (W.B.A.), J. Martin (Aston Villa), A.R. Scott (Wolves).
England XI: F. Broome (Aston Villa), J. Martin (Aston Villa).
All British XI: F. Broome (Aston Villa), G. Cummings (Aston Villa), D. Dearson (Birmingham), A. McNab (W.B.A.), J. Martin (Aston Villa), F. O'Donnell (Aston Villa).
Army: S. Cullis (Wolves, 5 apps).
RAF: R. King (Wolves).

1940-41
Football League XI: R. Dorsett (Wolves), T. Galley (Wolves), D. Westcott (Wolves).
British XI: S. Cullis (Wolves), D. Dearson (Birmingham).
Army: S. Cullis (Wolves, 7 apps).

John Martin (Aston Villa)

Alex Massie (Aston Villa)

1941-42
Football League XI: D. Dearson (Birmingham), F. Haycock (Aston Villa), L. Morgan (Walsall), R. Scott (Wolves).
Ireland XI: L. Kelly (Wolves).
Welsh XI: K. Kendrick (Birmingham), C. Sidlow (Wolves).
F.A. XI: F. Broome (Aston Villa), S. Cullis (Wolves), J. Martin (Aston Villa).
Army: S. Cullis (Wolves, 8 apps), F. Taylor (Wolves, 6 apps).
RAF: S. Butler (W.B.A.), W. Hughes (Birmingham, 2 apps), R. Shaw (Birmingham), C. Trigg (Birmingham).
Combined Services: R. King (Wolves).
Western Command: E. Robinson (Wolves), F. Taylor (Wolves).
Eastern Command: J. Martin (Aston Villa), F. Pincott (Wolves).
London Command: E. Jones (W.B.A.), G. Thompson (Aston Villa).
RAF (Amateur): B. Williams (Walsall).
Welsh Services: D. Witcomb (W.B.A.).
National Police: F. Harris (Birmingham).
Metropolitan Police: F. Harris (Birmingham, 2 apps), W.G. Richardson (W.B.A.).

1942-43
F.A. XI: F. Broome (Aston Villa), S. Cullis (Wolves), D. Dearson (Birmingham), J. Martin (Aston Villa), C. Sidlow (Wolves), F. Taylor (Wolves), D. Westcott (Wolves).
Welsh XI: D. Dearson (Birmingham), W. Hughes (Birmingham), G. Lowrie (Coventry).
Army: S. Cullis (Wolves, 7 apps), J. Mullen (Wolves, 5 apps), D. Westcott (Wolves, 4 apps).
RAF: S. Butler (W.B.A.), W. Hughes (Birmingham).
Western Command: F. Harris (Birmingham).
Eastern Command: T. Burden (Wolves).
Northern Command: J. Mullen (Wolves).
National Police: W.G. Richardson (W.B.A. 3 apps).
Police & Civil Defence XI: W.G. Richardson (W.B.A.)
London District: E. Jones (W.B.A.)
Civil Defence: W. G. Richardson (W.B.A., 2 apps).
Metropolitan Police: W.G. Richardson (W.B.A.).

Tom Galley (Wolves)

Bob King (Wolves)

1943-44
England XI: S. Cullis (Wolves), W. Elliott (W.B.A.), F. Taylor (Wolves).
Scotland XI: A. Massie (Aston Villa).
Army: S. Cullis (Wolves, 4 apps), W. Elliott (W.B.A. 2 apps), J. Mullen (Wolves), F. Taylor (Wolves, 4 apps), D. Westcott (Wolves).
Western Command: W. Elliott (W.B.A., 5 apps), F. Harris (Birmingham), H. Kinsell (W.B.A., 3 apps), F. Taylor (Wolves).
Northern Command: T Galley (Wolves, 3 apps), J. Mullen (Wolves, 3 apps), J. Rutherford (Aston Villa, 2 apps)
Eastern Command: C. Young (Coventry City).
Civil Defence: E. Callaghan (Aston Villa), W. G. Richardson (W.B.A.).
RAF: Strong (Walsall).
Combined Services: J. Martin (Aston Villa).
F.A. XI: S. Cullis (Wolves).
London District: E. Jones (W.B.A.), J. Martin (Aston Villa).
Police & Civil Defence: E. Callaghan (Aston Villa), G. Merrick (Birmingham).

Fred Harris (Birmingham)

Billy Hughes (Birmingham)

1944-45
F.A. XI: F. Broome (Aston Villa), H. Kinsell (W.B.A.), J. Martin (Aston Villa), G. Merrick (Birmingham), B. Williams (Walsall).
F.A. Services XI: W. Hughes (Birmingham), J. Mullen (Wolves).
Welsh XI: D. Dearson (Birmingham), A. Evans (W.B.A.), W. Hughes (Birmingham), C. Sidlow (Wolves).
Army: W. Elliott (W.B.A., 2 apps), F. Harris (Birmingham), H. Kinsell (W.B.A., 3 apps), J. Mullen (Wolves, 7 apps), F. Taylor (Wolves, 2 apps).
RAF: W. Hughes (Birmingham), B. Williams (Walsall, 5 apps).
Royal Navy: L. Latham (Aston Villa).
Western Command: W. Elliott (W.B.A., 4 apps), F. Harris (Birmingham, 3 apps), J. Hancocks (Walsall), F. Taylor (Wolves), W. Tudor (W.B.A.), W. Wright (Wolves).
Northern Command: J. Mullen (Wolves, 3 apps), J. Rutherford (Aston Villa), C. Sidlow (Wolves, 2 apps).
Eastern Command: H. Kinsell (W.B.A.)
Combined Services: J. Mullen (Wolves)
London District: E. Jones (W.B.A, 2 apps).
Police & Civil Defence: W.G. Richardson (W.B.A.)

1945-46
F.A. XI: W. Elliott (W.B.A.), F. Mitchell (Birmingham), L. Smith (Aston Villa), B. Williams (Wolves).
F.A. of Ireland: D. Walsh (W.B.A.)
Combined Services: H. Kinsell (W.B.A.), W. Wright (Wolves).
A.P.T.C. XI: G. Merrick (Birmingham), W. Wright (Wolves).

Facts and Figures

- Martin (Aston Villa) scored twice and Broome once in the England XI's 4-3 win over the Army at Selhurst Park in January 1940.
- Stan Cullis scored a rare goal for the Army in their 8-2 win over Allied Armies at Chelsea in March 1941.
- Dicky Dorsett (Wolves) netted twice for the Football League when the All British XI were defeated 9-7 at Anfield in April 1941.
- Villa's Frank Broome hit both goals for the F.A. XI in their 7-2 defeat by the RAF at Bristol in November 1941.
- Birmingham's Don Dearson, playing at inside-left, scored once in the Football League XI's 5-3 win over the Western Command side at Molineux in March 1942 — and he set up two of Dodd's three goals in that same match.
- Albion's W.G. Richardson and Fred Harris of Birmingham each scored twice for the Metropolitan Police in their 6-3 win over the Welsh Services at Cardiff in May 1942.
- Wolves' left-winger Jimmy Mullen scored in two successive matches for the Army in September 1942 — against the Irish League at Belfast on Scotland at Dumfries.
- Dennis Westcott (Wolves) struck home two of the three goals scored by the Army against the RAF at Leeds in December 1942. Two months later he whipped in a hat-trick as the Army (England) beat the Scottish Army 7-0 at Hampden Park infront of 30,000 spectators. Then, in April 1943, the Army XI slammed the luckless Norwegian Forces Select 11-0 and Westcott weighed in with a fourtimer.
- Albions W.G. Richardson fired home two smart goals for the National Police side at Wembley in May 1943 — but he still finished up a loser as the RAF won 4-3.
- Billy Elliott (W.B.A.) was a hat-trick hero at Stoke in March 1944 when he helped the Army beat an F.A. XI 5-2 before a 23,542 gate.
  Elliott was on target again a fortnight later when the Army beat the RAF 4-0 infront of 50,000 spectators in Edinburgh.
- Two goals by Elliott gave the Army victory (2-0) over an Army XI in Naples in May 1945.
- And the flying Albion winger was again a goalscorer for the F.A. XI who lost 5-3 to the A.P.T.C. XI at Wembley in April 1946 when the attendance was 90,000.

'W.G.' Richardson, centre-forward supreme, scored 100 "war" goals for West Bromwich Albion.

Stan Cullis, skipper and centre-half of Wolves and England, made only 24 war appearances for his club.

Frank Broome, utility forward of Aston Villa, netted 96 goals for the 'Villans' during the hostilities.

Points of Interest 1939-40

- Harry Jones (W.B.A.) scored in 11 successive Midland regional matches from 28th October to 30th December inclusive, to set a new club record. Jones finished with a total of 50 goals this season (42 in competitive matches).

- On 22nd May 1940, four League players: Frank Broome (Aston Villa), George Edwards (Aston Villa), Jimmy Duggan (W.B.A.) and Dennis Westcott (Wolves) were each paid £4.00 to turn-out for Chelmsford against Worcester City. (The maximum wage at the time was 30 shillings: £1.50!).

- The first transfer of the war took effect on 22nd November 1939 when Bob King, Northampton Town's outside-right, moved to Wolves for a ''substantial'' fee said to be £2,000.

- On 14th October 1939 Birmingham fielded two first teams: they lost 1-0 at Wolves and 3-2 at Stoke. Both were friendly matches.
West Bromwich Albion went even better — they played 2 games on each of three separate days: 7th and 14th October and 6th January. They won 5 and drew one, including an 11-1 victory over Burton Town.

- Tommy Crawley scored 8 goals in Coventry's record war win of 10-2 over Luton Town in March 1940 — and during that same month he netted a total of 14 goals out of City's tally of 30.

- Walsall played Luton Town four times in 1939-40 — and a total of 26 goals were scored in six hours of football.

Harry Hibbs (Birmingham).

Jimmy Mullen (Wolves).

- In April, 1940 goalkeeper Harry Hibbs of Birmingham and England retired. He later became manager of Walsall.

JUBILEE FUND MATCHES
Played 19th August 1939

Aston Villa 1 West Bromwich Albion 1
Attendance: 16,007

Coventry City 3 Birmingham 0
Attendance: 7,979

Stoke City 2 Wolves 4
Attendance: 5,289

* Dorsett scored a hat-trick for Wolves at Stoke.

- Jimmy Mullen celebrated his 17th birthday by helping Wolves beat Coventry City 3-0 on 6th January 1940. This was Mullen's first appearance for the club as a professional, having signed the appropriate forms just four hours before the kick-off.

- The average age of the Wolves team which played against Birmingham on 16th March 1940 was 19 years seven months.

- One of the first dismissals in wartime football was that of W.B.A. inside-forward Eddie Connelly who was sent-off against Coventry City on 23rd March 1940. In November of the following season he was again banished playing against Coventry — and was subsequently banned for life from 9th November 1940, only to be allowed to return on 25th October 1941.

1940-41

- On 28th December 1940 Birmingham, after losing 6-3 at Walsall on Christmas Day, announced that they were 'shutting up shop' and would no longer play competitive football, certainly not at St. Andrews. Luton Town replaced Blues in the Midland Cup.

- On 1st March 1941 Blues beat Luton 5-2 away — and they also entered the War Cup, replacing Coventry City.

- Charlie Rickards scored 3 goals in 3½ minutes for Mansfield Town against W.B.A. on 8th March 1941.

- Arthur Rowley, who, after the hostilities, went on to score a record 434 Football League goals, joined Manchester United at the age of 14 in 1940. He made his debut for the 'Reds' five days after his 15th birthday (26.4.41) at outside-right and his brother, Jack, played on the opposite flank. Arthur also guested for Wolves while playing for Blakenhall St. Luke's. He signed for W.B.A. as a professional in April 1944 after he had asked United to cancel his registration. Arthur, by now, had been converted into a centre-forward, but while guesting for Brighton and Crystal Palace he turned out at left-back. He served in Germany and Palestine during the war.

Jack Rowley

Arthur Rowley

- Albion and Walsall came face to face with each other on six occasions in 1940-41 — and between them the Baggies and the Saddlers rattled in 37 goals in nine hours of action.

- Thirteen goals were registered in the Walsall v Nottingham Forest game of 24th May 1941 — and seven days later another '13' were scored when Albion were hammered 10-3 by the Saddlers at Fellows Park. Jack Rowley hit 4 goals in each of those games for Walsall.

- Villa suffered their heaviest wartime defeat on 21st September 1940 when they crashed to Revo Electric, 8-4 infront of 1,500 spectators. Davis scored three for Villa — his first treble of the eleven he was to claim during the war.

- Albion lost the first leg of their Midland Cup tie against Notts County at Meadow Lane on 15th February 1941 by 4-0.
  In the return leg — at The Hawthorns seven days later — Albion won 5-0 to complete one of the greatest come-backs in competitive football.

- Tom Finney, who was to make such an impact on the English scene after the hostilities, made his debut for P.N.E. against Liverpool in August 1940 — and within a minute he was clattered by Stan Cullis, the Wolves centre-half, who was guesting for the Anfield club.

- On 3rd May 1941 Wolves players Jimmy Mullen and Billy Wright both 'guested' for Leicester City against Walsall in the Midland Cup Final (Leicester won 2-0).

- Walsall's best win in wartime was 11-4 — achieved against Notts County (home) on 9th November 1940, infront of just 427 fans — the lowest gate at Fellows Park during wartime. Jack Rowley and Ted Vinall each netted 4 goals apiece that day. Vinall's tally included a hat-trick of penalties in the second half.

- Twelve goals were scored in the Mansfield v Walsall Regional South match at Field Mill on 26th October 1940. The final score was a 6-6 draw and Rickards hit 4 of Mansfield's goals.

Tom Finney

1941-42

- On 27th September 1941 Wolves fielded their youngest-ever first team. The average age was 17 and Ashton was the veteran of the side at 18 years 6 months.

- On 25th October 1941, England beat Wales 2-1 at bomb-damaged St. Andrews. The gate limit was set at 25,000 and admission to the ground was by ticket only: 1/6d and 10/6d; Don Dearson (Blues) missed a penalty for the Welsh.

- Harold White, the West Bromwich Albion full-back, was awarded the Military Medal on 21st March 1942. He was the second professional footballer to be decorated in wartime.

- In 1941-42 Birmingham opted out of the Regional League Competition and decided to play friendly matches — when they could put together a side!

- The League Championship of 1941-42 was completed on Christmas Day and because of unplayed matches, the final table was calculated on the average number of points which would have been gained had teams played the maximum number of 18 matches. Thus, Leicester City won the title by 0.1 of a point from the rather annoyed West Bromwich Albion.

- Many football grounds suffered severe bomb damage during the early part of the war — and one of the worst to suffer was St. Andrews, home of Birmingham.

- At the end of the 1941-42 season Wolves drew 1-1 with Brentford at Stamford Bridge in the meeting of the respective North and South Wartime Cup winners. Mullen scored for Wolves but the Midland club finished with only 10 men. It was a blazing hot day with the temperature nearing the mid 80's (in the shade). Eric 'Ned' Robinson, the Wolves right-half, collapsed just before half-time and again 15 minutes from the end, apparently with concussion. At the time weather conditions were forbidden to be released 'over the air' — so it was three years before the story that Robinson was suffering from sun-stroke could be revealed. Later Robinson tragically lost his life on military service when he was drowned on exercises.

- On 3rd January 1942, Walsall suffered their heaviest wartime defeat when they lost 8-0 away to Stoke City in a 'League Cup' match.

- Dicky Davis netted 30 goals for Aston Villa in 1941-42, including a sixtimer v Worcester City (away) on 1st November.

- Villa beat Hednesford Town 5-0 at home (Solihull) on 23rd May 1942 to carry off the Keys Cup. Albert Kerr scored a hat-trick but there were only 1,200 present to see the action.
  Villa's team was: Wakeman; Potts, Cummings; Massie, Callaghan, Iverson; Kerr, Canning, Davis, Goffin and Edwards.

- A fortnight earlier — on 9th May 1942 — Villa defeated Worcester City (home) 4-2 to win the Birmingham League Cup. Their line-up for this final was: Wakeman; Potts, Cummings; Kerr, Callaghan, Iverson; Cooper, Houghton, Davis, Carswell and Goffin.

- Villa also took the Birmingham and District League Championship in 1941-42 to complete the treble!

- Aston Villa's best win in wartime came in March 1942 when they crushed R.A.F. (Lichfield) at home by 19-2 in a Birmingham and District League match. Just 750 spectators saw Frank Broome, Billy Goffin and Harry Parkes hit 4 goals apiece as Villa 'flew' home in style!

- In that same season (17th January 1942) Villa whipped R.A.F. (Hednesford) 14-1 in a Birmingham Cup tie — and this time Alex Massie hit 5 and Broome 4.

CUP JOY FOR WOLVES

Tom Galley, receiving the League (North) War Cup, after Wolves had defeated Sunderland over two legs in the 1942 Final. Pictured with Tom is Wolves' manager, Major Frank Buckley.

- On 21st January 1942 the main stand at St. Andrews, home of Birmingham, went up in flames after a fireman threw 'petrol' on to a brazier! He had picked up a bucket thinking it was full of water . . . !

- Albion's flying winger Billy Elliott scored in eleven consecutive matches during 1941-42 to equal the club record set by Harry Jones in 1939-40.

- West Bromwich Albion scored eight goals in 32 minutes of their home game against Luton Town on 22nd November 1941. They won the match 10-1.

- West Bromwich Albion scored eight goals in 32 minutes of their home game against Luton Town on 22nd November 1941. They won the match 10-1.

- Albion had been involved in another high-scoring game against Cardiff City on 30th August 1941, when in their 6-3 win they netted five goals in the first eleven minutes.

- On 13th December 1941 Dennis Westcott hit six goals for Wolves against Nottingham Forrest.

- Wolves won the Football League North Cup in season 1941-42 and a record wartime gate of 43,038 packed Molineux to see the second leg of the final against Sunderland.

- In a friendly match between West Bromwich Albion and Birmingham at The Hawthorns on 30th May 1942, both sides were awarded two penalties. Albion won the game 4-1.

- In a 1st leg Cup game on 4th April 1942, Albion were 5-0 down to Stoke City, but they recovered to reduce the arrears to 5-3. In the return fixture at The Hawthorns 48 hours later Albion won 6-1 for an aggregate 9-6 victory — and so achieved yet another of soccer's greatest fight-backs.

1942-43

- On 26th September 1942, Ernie 'Mush' Callaghan (Aston Villa) was awarded the British Empire Medal for gallantry during an air raid. Callaghan was serving in the Police Reserve Force.

- George Edwards played for Aston Villa against Walsall on 26th September 1942 with his arm encased in plaster.

- On 31st October 1942, after a lengthy meeting, the F.A. made an official statement concerning Cameron Campbell Buchanan, who, on 26th September 1942, had played for Wolves against W.B.A. at the age of just 14 years 57 days . . . the youngest-ever footballer in Britain to participate in a competitive match. Buchanan did not play for Wolves again until 15th April 1944 when he was still only 15!. The F.A. stated that Wolves were not wrong to play the boy but it was not in the best interests of the game that so young a lad should be taken so far from his home to play in League football.

- George Cummings of Aston Villa, was suspended sine die from 18th January 1943 following incidents 'of a serious nature' in the Leicester v Aston Villa match on 25th December 1942.

- A crowd of 105,145 assembled at Hampden Park on 17th April 1943 to watch England thrash Scotland 4-0. During the course of the game Stan Cullis, the Wolves and England centre-half, was injured in an "off the ball" incident involving Wallace of Clyde. A Scottish F.A. official said afterwards: "Wallace would never play for Scotland again!" (he didn't).

Cameron Buchanan (Wolves).

- Jack Smith, the Chelsea full-back, who guested for W.B.A., slipped on a Wolverhampton kerbstone in the war and a bus (driven by a Wolves supporter) ran over his foot. His thick sole, however, minimised the injury but the accident ended Smith's playing career. After the war he became Manager of Albion.
Smith had earlier played 27 games for Wolves between 1931 and 1934.

- George Lowrie hit two fourtimers for Coventry in 1942-43 — both at home: v Northampton Town on 10th October (won 5-0) and against Notts County on 24th April (won 7-0).

- Walsall utilised a total of 51 players in their 34 matches in season 1942-43.

- On 21st November 1942 Jack Rowley (Manchester United) who was guesting for Wolves, scored all eight goals in the Wanderers' emphatic victory over Derby County — all from the wing position!
Eight months earlier (in March 1942) he had registered a fivetimer for Wolves against Everton.

- At the end of this fourth 'wartime' season, it was announced that Wolves had lost a total of £24,763 since the start of the hostilities — £17,717 in 1939-40, £4,846 in 1940-41 (when they didn't even play), £979 in 1941-42 and £1,221 in 1942-43.

- During the 1942-43 campaign Lawrie Kelly (aged 17) skippered Wolves — probably the youngest ever captain of the club.

1943-44

- On 20th August 1943 the 'Sine Die' suspension imposed on 'Mush' Callaghan (Villa) was lifted by the F.A.

- Aston Villa were leading Walsall by 4-0 at Villa Park in a Regional League game on 2nd October 1943. But in the remaining 15 minutes the Saddlers stormed back to force a 4-4 draw, Gilbert Alsop scoring twice.

- On Christmas Day 1943 Coventry striker Tommy Crawley hit five of his side's eight goals against West Bromwich Albion.

- On 2nd October 1943 Alan Steen, who had made his debut for Wolves as a 16-year-old in 1938-39, was reported 'missing' after a bombing raid over Germany. He was captured by the enemy and spent the remainder of the war as a P.O.W. in Stalag IV 3.
On returning to England after the hostilities, Steen went on to play League Football for Luton, Aldershot, Rochdale and Carlisle United, quitting the bigtime in 1952.

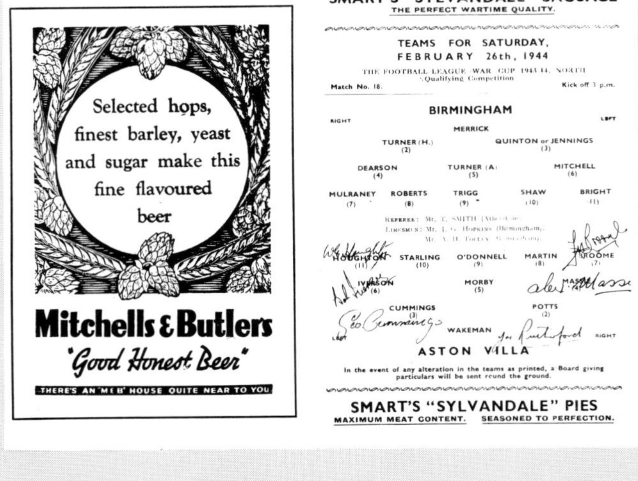

1943-44
CUP DOUBLE

Villa Take Cup From Blackpool

By BERT FOGG

ASTON VILLA . . . . . . 4 BLACKPOOL 2

ASTON VILLA won a remarkable and memorable game in the second leg of the League North Cup Final at Villa Park, and so checked the run of successes achieved by Blackpool in this competition.

The game was a magnificent one to watch. It was sensational in every respect, and produced many good thrills. It was a very fast game, and the spectators were kept on tip-toe with excitement throughout.

Bob Iverson 1943-44

A little too much keeness was manifest at times, but on the whole it was fought in very good spirit. The Villa commenced under the handicap of a goal down because of their 2-1 defeat at Blackpool in the first leg.

Deficit Wiped Out

They wiped this deficit off in the first minute and from then on it was a pulsating affair. First one team and then the other attacked with great determination. Neither side being able to claim territorial advantage for any length of time.

The forward play of both teams was wonderful and sometimes it appeared that all the half-backs were playing in the front-line in addition to the forwards.

Each set of half-backs were in excellent form, consequently, the attacks on goals were fast and furious.

Several times the goalkeeper was drawn out of position and goals were saved by full-backs dropping from nowhere and heading or kicking shots out from underneath the bar.

The respective defences had a gruelling time and the surprise is not at the many goals scored, but that many more weren't scored. Mistakes were made but the defences stood up well to their difficult task.

Potts was ever a shining light in the Villa defence, while Kinsell stood out for Blackpool. On the whole the Villa were the better balanced team and merited their win through the sterling work of the half-backs.

The Villa did not make the mistake of easing up near the end as they did at Blackpool, and we waited for the characteristic Blackpool revival near the end, but alas it never came.

It is impossible to imagine a more sensational start to a game especially a Cup Final. Two goals were scored in the first 75 seconds and two more before the game was 15 minutes old.

I did not think that any of the first three should have counted, as they were all suspect in character. The first was scored by Broome for the Villa from a pass by Iverson, who appeared to be well offside. Time: 40 seconds.

Almost from the restart Blackpool attacked and Dodds shot, and again I thought his position was offside. His shot was knocked out by Wakeman and it went to Dix whose shot entered the net after hitting Cummings.

In the 10th minute Villa took the lead through Edwards. Here, again I thought his goal should not have been allowed, as it appeared to me a case of handling which produced the goal.

No Doubts

Blackpool equalised through Pearson five minutes later, and this time there was no doubt about the legitimacy of the goal. It was a good one in every respect.

The Villa regained the lead after 38 minutes. Houghton sent in a very fast shot which Savage could only knock down and, from the rebound Iverson sailed in to score.

Just five minutes had gone in the second half when Villa scored again to give them a two-goal lead in the two games. Broome scored this goal after good work by Houghton and this proved to be the winner.

ASTON VILLA — Wakeman; Potts, Cummings; Massie, Callaghan, Starling; Broome, Edwards, Parkes, Iverson, Houghton.

BLACKPOOL — Savage; Pope, Kinsell; Johnstone, Hayward, Jones; Matthews, Dix, Dodds, Finan, Pearson.

Referee: E. R. MacLachlan.

ALBION WIN MARATHON MATCH

Victory Snatched in Amazing Scene

Nottm. F. 3, W.B. Albion 4.

Sensation followed sensation in the second "leg" of the Midland Cup final between Albion and the Forest. It was a marathon affair, actual play lasting only a minute short of two hours. During the whole time a record war-time crowd of 14,438 — included in which was a small but vociferous band of Albion supporters — was kept in a roar of excitement.

When Forest scored their third goal in the nineteenth minute of 20 minutes' extra time, a large section of the crowd invaded the pitch and began to carry the Forest players towards the grandstand to have the cup presented. They thought the match was over . . . but the referee thought differently. His watch told him that there was still nearly two minutes left for play, so the police cleared the pitch and the game went on. From midfield, Albion went clean through the Forest defence and Acquaroff scored.

With extra time exhausted — and the players not far off being in the same state after a terrific gruelling — the referee ordered that the match must go on until a deciding goal was scored. It came in the ninth minute of "extra" extra time, Clarke being the marksman.

In the early stages of the game Albion were in a subdued mood, and at one time it seemed that the Forest had the game well in hand. Forest's forward line was strengthened by the inclusion of Steele (Stoke City) and in goal they had Middleton (Chesterfield), in place of Platts, who dislocated his shoulder at the Hawthorns on the previous Saturday.

The teams started all-square, the result of the first "leg" being 2-2, but Forest soon went ahead with goals by Steele and Johnstone. Near half-time Albion's cup-fighting traditions began to assert themselves. A dogged rally brought a goal by Acquaroff, and midway through the second half Hodgetts headed a brilliant equaliser after neat work by Clarke. Dulson scored the Forest's third goal in extra time.

The Lord Mayor of Nottingham presented the cup to McNab, Albion's captain. The trophy was provided by the Birmingham County F.A., and the winners retain it outright. In lieu of medals, the victors and runners-up received savings certificates.

Albion's team was: Heath; Southam, Smith; Millard, Gripton, McNab; Heaselgrave, Clarke, Acquaroff, Evans (C), Hodgetts.

Bill Morris (Wolves)

Ray Barlow (Albion)

1944-45

- Aston Villa beat an Edinburgh Select XI 4-3 in a friendly at Tynecastle Park on 5th August 1944. Frank Broome (2), Bob Iverson and Eric Houghton scored for Villa.
- Villa won the Football League (North) War Cup in 1944 and on 21st October of that year the club held a 'mock' auction for that same trophy. Over £450 was raised for the Red Cross funds — but the Cup itself remained at Villa Park, the 'winner' John Wright handing it back!
- On 24th March 1945 Wolves beat Aston Villa 2-1 at Villa Park — the deciding goal coming from a penalty, converted by 20 year-old Jimmy Alderton, his first ever-spot-kick for the Wanderers.
- Coventry suffered their heaviest wartime defeat in May 1945 when they crashed 9-2 at Aston Villa.
- In January 1945 Albion's reserve XI beat Smethwick Highfield 17-0 in a friendly match at The Hawthorns, and Ray Barlow, later to win a full England cap, scored a 'double' hat-trick while Tommy Bowen netted seven goals.
- Wolves beat Birmingham 1-0 at Molineux in a 2nd Round, 2nd leg League Cup (N) match on 14th April 1945. The winning goal, scored by Bill Morris, arrived in the 63rd minute of the added extra 'extra time' period, of a game which lasted 153 minutes, the referee calling a halt when Morris netted. The game started at 3 o'clock and finished at 5.45pm!

1945-46

- Alex Massie played his last game for Aston Villa on 1st September 1945. He then 'hung up' his boots to take over as manager at Villa Park.
- On 6th October 1945, Ted Duckhouse set Blues on their way to a convincing 8-0 victory over Tottenham Hotspur by scoring the opening goal of the game from fully 50 yards.
- Harry Storer was officially appointed manager of Birmingham on 1st June 1945.
- Aston Villa ran up a sequence of 11 successive wins from 20th October 1945 to 25th December 1945 inclusive. Birmingham registered 18 consecutive home victories at St. Andrews from 3rd September 1945 to 9th March 1946.
- It was recorded that Wolves had a total of 91 of their players on active service during the 1939-45 wartime period. (Crystal Palace topped the poll with 98).
- On 22nd April 1946 Walsall's best crowd of the 'war' — 13,146 — witnessed the cup game against Northampton Town at Fellows Park which Walsall won 3-1.
- In 1945-46 Villa had to win both their remaining two matches to pip neighbours Birmingham City for the Football League South Championship. They couldn't manage it — drawing 2-2 at Coventry and beating Millwall 2-0. Blues won the title on goal-average: 96-45 to Villa's 106-58. Both teams finished with 61 points, one more than Charlton Athletic.
- George Edwards top-scored for Aston Villa in 1945-46 with a total of 43 goals. He netted in 11 consecutive matches: from 20th October to 25th December inclusive.
- When 'wartime' football ended, it was revealed that Aston Villa had only used three 'guest' players — Dicky Davis (Sunderland), Vic Potts (Doncaster) and Bob Scott (Wolves). Potts later joined Villa on a permanent basis. Davis recorded 11 hat-tricks for Villa between 1940 and 1943.
- Villa's average League attendance for 1945-46 (21 home matches played) was 32,981. Taking into consideration 4 F.A. Cup ties at Villa Park, the overall average that season (25 games fulfilled) was 34,927 — boosted no doubt, by a record 76,588 turn-out for the 6th Round F.A. Cup clash with Derby County on 2nd March.

Back row (left to right): Harry Kinsell, Cecil Shaw, Harold White, Jim Sanders, George Tranter, Len Millard.

Front row: Billy Elliott, Ike Clarke, Bobby Newsome, Doug Witcomb, Eddie Connelly and Stan Butler.

Old Rivals

George Cummings (left) of Aston Villa shaking hands with his fellow skipper, Fred Harris of Birmingham

Results, Scorers, Attendances.

This section gives you all the results, goalscorers, attendances and seasonal appearance totals of the six Midland clubs.

Aston Villa

Season 1939-40

FOOTBALL LEAGUE DIVISION 1

Aug	26	(h)	Middlesbrough	W	2-0	Martin, Edwards	36,038
	28	(h)	Everton	L	1-2	Cummings	29,359
Sep	2	(a)	Derby County	L	0-1		7,996

Appearances (League): J.P. Allen 3, F.H. Broome 3, E. Callaghan 3, W.J. Carey 1, G. Cummings 3, G.R. Edwards 3, F. Haycock 1, R.T. Iverson 3, J.R. Martin 3, A. Massie 3, F. O'Donnell 3, J. Rutherford 2, R.W. Starling 2 — **Total 33.**

Goalscorers (League): Cummings 1, Edwards 1, Martin 1 — **Total 3.**

RECORD

P	W	D	L	F	A
3	1	0	2	3	3

Season 1940-41

BIRMINGHAM & DISTRICT LEAGUE

Sep	14	(a)	Hednesford	L	1-6	Goffin	2,000
	21	(a)	Revo Elect	L	4-8	Davis 3, Goffin	1,500
Oct	12	(h)	RAF (Cosford)	L	0-1		1,000
Nov	9	(h)	Wellington	L	1-4	Houghton	2,500
	16	(a)	RAF (Cosford)	L	1-3	Shell	700
Dec	14	(h)	RAF (Hednesfd)	L	3-4	Goffin 2, Edwards	2,000
	21	(a)	Worcester	L	2-3	Davis, Goffin	3,500
Feb	15	(h)	RAF (Bridgnrth)	W	3-1	Davis 3	1,000
	22	(a)	Revo Elect	W	4-1	Bate, Davis 3	500
Mar	1	(h)	RAF (Hednesfd)	W	5-1	Bate, Shell, Parkes, Davis 2	1,200
	15	(a)	Worcester	L	3-5	Davis, Carter, Brown (og)	3,000
Apr	5	(h)	RAF (Bradford)	W	8-1	Davis, Broome 3, Goffin 2, Parkes, Bate	1,000
	12	(a)	Wellington	L	2-4	Davis, Goffin	2,500
	14	(a)	W.B.A.	L	3-4	Edwards, Broome, Haycock	4,549
	26	(h)	W.B.A.	W	6-1	Davis 3, Goffin, Kerr, Martin	3,700
May	3	(a)	Hednesford	L	0-2		1,500

BIRMINGHAM LEAGUE CUP

Oct	26	(a)	Worcester	L	0-2		2,000
Nov	2	(h)	Worcester	D	2-2	Houghton, Bate	1,500

WORCESTER CUP

Dec	7	(a)	Revo Elect	L	1-2	Parkes	500

WORCESTER INFIRMARY CUP

May	10	(a)	Worcester	L	1-2	Parkes	2,500

Appearances (League & Cup): Airey 1, Aston 9, J. Barker 6, J. Bate 11, S. Batty 1, Beresford 1, G. Billingsley 6, F.H. Broome 5, E. Callaghan 5, Carter 1, G. Cummings 6, R.D. Davis 14*, Devonport 1, G.R. Edwards 5, Gibbons 1, W.C. Goffin 16, F. Haycock 1, Hickman 10, W.E. Houghton 8, R. Iverson 2, A.W. Kerr 9, Knight 10, King 1, Lowry 1, Lunn 1, J.R. Martin 4, A. Massie 4, A. Moss 7, Neville 1, H. Parkes 15, Parsons 1, Perry 2, V.E. Potts 16*, J. Rutherford 1, F.H. Shell 12, Spencer 1, Vinall 1, A. Wakeman 13, R.E. York 10 — **Total 220.** ** Guest player.*

Goalscorers (L & C): Davis 18, Goffin 9, Bate 4, Broome 4, Parkes 4, Edwards 2, Houghton 2, Shell 2, Carter 1, Haycock 1, Kerr 1, Martin 1, opponent 1 — **Total 50.**

RECORD

P	W	D	L	F	A
20	5	1	14	50	57

Back Row (left to right)—H. Bourne (trainer), Massie, Callaghan, Biddleston, Iverson, Cummings, J. Hogan (manager). *Front Row*—Broome, Haycock, Allen, Shell, Starling, Houghton.

Season 1941-42

BIRMINGHAM & DISTRICT LEAGUE

Sep	6	(a)	Hednesford	W	3-0	Davis 3	1,000
	13	(h)	RAF (Hednesfd)	W	2-1	Houghton, Davis	1,500
	20	(a)	Revo Elect	W	5-1	Davis 2, Martin, Pearce, Houghton	600
	27	(h)	Wellington	W	5-1	Davis 3, Parkes, Martin	2,000
Oct	4	(a)	Wellington	L	0-5		2,000
	11	(h)	W.B.A.	L	2-3	Davis, Parkes	5,500
	18	(h)	RAF (Cosford)	W	3-0	Davis 2, Goffin	1,000
Nov	1	(a)	Worcester	W	8-1	Davis 6, Parkes, Bate	3,000
Dec	25	(a)	W.B.A.	W	2-0	Haycock, Edwards	5,178
Jan	3	(a)	Wolves	W	3-1	Broome 2, Iverson	6,000
	10	(h)	Hednesford	W	8-0	Broome, Parkes, Iverson 2, Goffin 2, Houghton 2	2,000
Feb	14	(h)	RAF (Hednesfd)	W	7-0	Kerr 3, Broome, Edwards 2, Houghton	1,000
	21	(h)	Revo Elect	W	3-0	Broome 3	850
Mar	24	(h)	RAF (Lichfield)	W	19-2	Broome 4, Parkes 4, Goffin 4, Kerr 2, Houghton 2, Cummings 2, Iverson	750
Apr	11	(h)	Worcester	W	2-0	Kerr, Broome	1,500
	18	(h)	RAF (Lichfield)	W	9-0	Canning 3, Kerr, Edwards 2, Goffin 2, Houghton	600
	25	(h)	RAF (Cosford)	D	0-0		400
May	16	(h)	Wolves	W	6-1	Houghton 2, Iverson, Kerr, Davis, Goffin	3,000

WORCESTER CUP

Dec	13	(h)	Revo Elect	L	1-2	Iverson	200

WORCESTER INFIRMARY CUP

May	2	(a)	Worcester	W	3-0	Goffin 2, Davis	1,200

Aston Villa

BIRMINGHAM LEAGUE CUP

Nov	8	(h)	Wellington	W	5-0	Davis 2, Martin, Houghton 2	800
	22	(a)	Wellington	L	1-2	Davis	1,900
Jan	17	(h)	RAF (Hednesfd)	W	14-1	Massie 5, Broome 4, Houghton 2, Parkes 2, Kerr	1,000
	31	(h)	Hednesford	W	3-2	Broome 2, Preston (og)	1,200
May	9	(h)	Worcester	W	4-2	Goffin 2, Davis, Houghton	1,000

KEYS CUP

Dec	6	(h)	Worcester	W	6-0	Davis 4, Goffin, Smith (og)	1,000
	24	(a)	Worcester	W	4-1	Davis 2, Parkes, Cottrill (og)	1,200
Feb	28	(a)	Revo Elect	W	2-1	Potts, Kerr	400
May	23	(h)	Hednesford	W	5-0	Kerr 3, Goffin 2	1,200

Appearances (League & Cup): Aston 2, J. Bate 18, Bentley 2, F.H. Broome 10, E. Callaghan 28, L. Canning 3, Carswell 1, Cooper 2, L. Croom 1, G. Cummings 28, R.D. Davis 18*, G.R. Edwards 4, W.C. Goffin 17, F. Haycock 1, Hickman 1, W.E. Houghton 23, R.T. Iverson 22, A.W. Kerr 26, Lunn 2, J.R. Martin 8, A. Massie 20, H. Parkes 23, Pearce 3, V.E. Potts 25*, J. Rutherford 4, R.W. Starling 1, Vinall 2, A. Wakeman 24 — **Total 319.** * *Guest player.*

Goalscorers (L & C): Davis 30, Broome 18, Goffin 17, Houghton 15, Kerr 13, Parkes 11, Iverson 6, Edwards 5, Massie 5, Canning 3, Martin 3, opponents 3, Cummings 2, Bate 1, Haycock 1, Pearce 1, Potts 1 — **Total 135.**

RECORD

P	W	D	L	F	A
29	24	1	4	135	27

Season 1942-43

FOOTBALL LEAGUE NORTH 1st CHAMPIONSHIP

Aug	29	(h)	Wolves	W	2-0	Parkes, Edwards	15,000
Sep	5	(a)	Wolves	W	2-1	Goffin, Cummings	8,000
	12	(a)	Coventry	L	1-2	Broome	14,720
	19	(h)	Coventry	D	1-1	Houghton	16,000
	26	(h)	Walsall	D	2-2	Broome, Haycock	7,550
Oct	3	(a)	Walsall	L	0-3		4,500
	10	(a)	W.B.A.	L	2-6	Houghton, Haycock	10,326
	17	(h)	W.B.A.	W	8-2	Houghton 3, Davis 2, Parkes 2, Broome	12,000
	24	(h)	Stoke City	W	4-0	Haycock 2, Parkes, Edwards	10,000
	31	(a)	Stoke City	L	0-1		6,000
Nov	7	(a)	Northampton	W	5-3	Haycock, Parkes, Houghton 2, Davis	4,000
	14	(h)	Northampton	W	4-1	Parkes, Houghton, Broome 2	4,800
	21	(h)	Birmingham	W	2-1	Davis 2	15,000
	28	(a)	Birmingham	L	1-2	Edwards	15,000
Dec	5	(a)	Derby County	L	2-4	Edwards, Parkes	7,000
	12	(h)	Derby County	W	2-0	Broome 2	7,000
	19	(h)	Leicester	W	4-2	Broome, Houghton 3	4,700
	25	(a)	Leicester	W	5-2	Kerr 2, Broome 2, Edwards	9,000

FOOTBALL LEAGUE WAR CUP (QUALIFYING ROUNDS)

Dec	26	(h)	Wolves	W	1-0	Edwards	20,000
Jan	2	(a)	Wolves	W	4-0	Broome 3, Davis	6,000
	9	(a)	Stoke City	L	0-1		3,000
	16	(h)	Stoke City	W	3-0	Edwards 2, Broome	7,000
	23	(h)	W.B.A.	L	3-5	Broome, Iverson, Davis	12,000
	30	(a)	W.B.A.	L	1-2	Broome	13,200
Feb	6	(a)	Northampton	L	1-2	Davis	6,000
	13	(h)	Northampton	W	2-1	Parkes, Haycock	7,000
	20	(h)	Walsall	W	2-1	Haycock, Houghton	12,000
	27	(a)	Walsall	W	4-1	Davis 3, Kerr	7,000

FOOTBALL LEAGUE WAR CUP (PROPER)

Mar	6	(h)	Wolves	W	5-2	Davis, Houghton 3, Broome	25,000
	13	(a)	Wolves	W	5-3	Houghton, Davis 3, Haycock	15,000
	20	(a)	Stoke City	W	3-1	Davis 2, Houghton	15,000
	27	(h)	Stoke City	W	2-0	Edwards, Houghton	20,000
Apr	3	(a)	Bristol City	D	0-0		24,650
	10	(h)	Bristol City	W	2-1	Houghton 2	30,000
	17	(a)	Blackpool	L	1-3	Davis	28,000
	24	(h)	Blackpool	W	2-1	Callaghan, Iverson	50,000

FOOTBALL LEAGUE NORTH 2nd CHAMPIONSHIP

Apr	26	(h)	Birmingham	W	1-0	Iverson	5,000
May	1	(h)	W.B.A.	L	2-6	Haycock, Edwards	5,163

Appearances (League & Cup): J. Bate 2, G. Billingsley 2, F.H. Broome 30, E. Callaghan 31, G. Cummings 22, R.D. Davis 16*, G.R. Edwards 24, L.L. Godfrey 4, W.C. Goffin 6, R. Gutteridge 16, F. Haycock 25, W.E. Houghton 33, R.T. Iverson 29, A.W. Kerr 6, J.R. Martin 6, A. Massie 32, H.A. Parkes 26, V.E. Potts 34*, F.H. Shell 4, R.W. Starling 34, A. Wakeman 36 — **Total 418.** * *Guest player.*

Goalscorers (L & C): Houghton 20, Broome 17, Davis 18, Edwards 10, Parkes 8, Haycock 9, Iverson 3, Kerr 3, Callaghan 1, Cummings 1, Goffin 1 — **Total 91.**

RECORD

P	W	D	L	F	A
38	23	3	12	91	63

Season 1943-44

FOOTBALL LEAGUE (NORTH) FIRST CHAMPIONSHIP

Aug	28	(a)	Stoke City	W	2-0	Edwards, Broome	6,000
Sep	4	(h)	Stoke City	W	2-1	Houghton (pen), Broome	15,000
	11	(a)	Wolves	W	4-2	Edwards, Houghton, Broome 2	10,000
	18	(h)	Wolves	W	4-1	Broome 2, Starling, Houghton	14,500
	25	(a)	Walsall	W	2-0	Broome, Houghton (pen)	7,000
Oct	2	(h)	Walsall	D	4-4	Broome, Houghton 2, Starling	15,000
	9	(h)	Coventry C	D	0-0		15,000
	16	(a)	Coventry C	W	1-0	Haycock	14,014
	23	(h)	W.B.A.	W	3-1	Davis, Broome, Houghton	19,000
	30	(a)	W.B.A.	L	4-5	Broome 2, Haycock, Iverson	23,550
Nov	6	(h)	Northampton T	W	4-0	Broome 2, Houghton, Haycock	14,000
	13	(a)	Northampton T	L	0-5		6,000
	20	(a)	Birmingham	L	1-2	Houghton	20,000
	27	(h)	Birmingham	W	3-0	O'Donnell 2, Broome	15,000
Dec	4	(h)	Derby County	L	0-1		12,000
	11	(a)	Derby County	D	3-3	Canning 2, Houghton	10,000
	18	(a)	Leicester C	W	3-1	Parkes 2, Houghton	5,000
	25	(h)	Leicester C	W	3-1	Houghton 2 (1 pen), Broome	10,000

Aston Villa

FOOTBALL LEAGUE (NORTH) SECOND CHAMPIONSHIP

Dec	16	(h)	Northampton T	W	2-1	Iverson, Houghton	14,000
Jan	1	(a)	Northampton T	W	2-1	O'Donnell, Broome	8,000
	8	(a)	Stoke City	L	3-6	O'Donnell, Haycock, Houghton	16,492
	15	(h)	Stoke City	L	0-2		32,000
	22	(a)	Wolves	W	4-0	Starling, Martin, O'Donnell, Broome	12,000
	29	(h)	Wolves	W	3-1	Goffin, Broome (pen), McLean (og)	16,000
Feb	5	(h)	Coventry C	W	4-0	O'Donnell, Broome 2, Starling	12,000
	12	(a)	Coventry C	L	0-2		15,770
	19	(a)	Birmingham	D	1-1	Iverson	18,000
	26	(h)	Birmingham	L	1-2	Broome	21,000
Mar	4	(a)	Stoke City	W	5-4	Martin, Broome 2, Houghton 2	11,508
	11	(h)	Stoke City	W	3-0	Houghton 2, Broome	22,000
	18	(a)	Coventry C	W	2-1	Iverson, Broome	23,664
	25	(h)	Coventry C	W	2-1	Broome, Guttridge	29,000
Apr	10	(h)	W.B.A.	W	4-1	Broome 3, Edwards	15,000

FOOTBALL LEAGUE (NORTH) CUP

Apr	1	(h)	Bath City	W	1-0	O'Donnell	29,488
	8	(a)	Bath City	D	3-3	Parkes 2, Iverson	15,597
	15	(h)	Sheffield U	W	3-2	Iverson 2, Houghton	40,000
	22	(a)	Sheffield U	D	2-2	Broome, Parkes	48,000
	29	(a)	Blackpool	L	1-2	Goffin	28,000
May	6	(h)	Blackpool	W	4-2	Broome 2, Edwards, Iverson	54,824

Aston Villa, winners of the Football League North Cup, met Charlton Athletic, Southern Cup winners, in a challenge match at Stamford Bridge on 20th May 1944. Villa's scorer in the 1-1 draw was Eric Houghton. Team: Wakeman; Potts, Cummings, Massie, Callaghan, Starling, Broome, Edwards, Parkes, Iverson, Houghton. *Attendance: 38,540.*

Appearances (League & Cup): G. Billingsley 3, F.H. Broome 41, E. Callaghan 20, L. Canning 2, G. Cummings 37, R.D. Davis 5*, G.R. Edwards 15, L.L Godfrey 2, W.C. Goffin 5, R. Guttridge 9, F. Haycock 22, W.E. Houghton 37, R.T. Iverson 40, J.R. Martin 6, A. Massie 37, J.H. Morby 19, F. O'Donnell 14, H. Parkes 18, V.E. Potts 41*, R.W. Starling 40, A. Wakeman 38 — **Total 451.** * *Guest player.*

Goalscorers (L & C): Broome 30, Houghton 22, Iverson 8, O'Donnell 7, Edwards 4, Haycock 4, Parkes 4, Starling 4, Goffin 3, Canning 2, Martin 2, opponents 2, Davis 1, Guttridge 1 — **Total 94.**

RECORD

P	W	D	L	F	A
40	24	7	9	94	62

Harry Parkes

Ronnie Starling

Eric Houghton

Villa's Wartime Cup winning team v Blackpool in 1944 was:

1st leg: Wakeman; Potts (Doncaster), Cummings; Massie, Callaghan, Iverson; Broome, Edwards, Parkes, Starling, Goffin.

2nd leg: Starling played at left-half, Iverson at inside-left and Houghton on the left-wing.

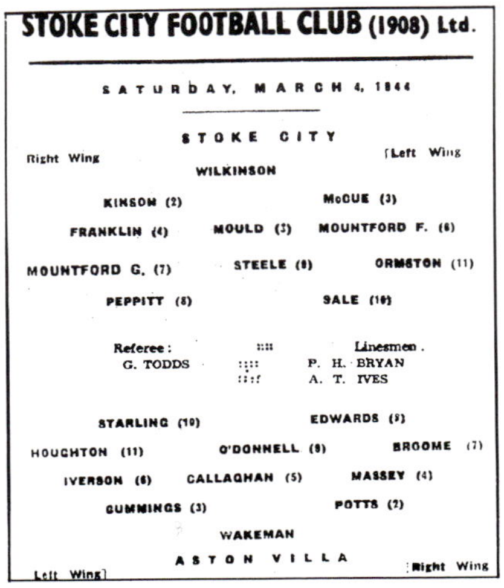

STOKE CITY FOOTBALL CLUB (1908) Ltd.

SATURDAY, MARCH 4, 1944

STOKE CITY

Right Wing — Left Wing

WILKINSON

KINSON (2) — McCUE (3)

FRANKLIN (4) — MOULD (5) — MOUNTFORD F. (6)

MOUNTFORD G. (7) — STEELE (9) — ORMSTON (11)

PEPPITT (8) — SALE (10)

Referee: G. TODDS

Linesmen. P. H. BRYAN, A. T. IVES

STARLING (10) — EDWARDS (8)

HOUGHTON (11) — O'DONNELL (9) — BROOME (7)

IVERSON (6) — CALLAGHAN (5) — MASSEY (4)

CUMMINGS (3) — POTTS (2)

WAKEMAN

ASTON VILLA

Left Wing — Right Wing

Aston Villa

Season 1944-45

FOOTBALL LEAGUE (NORTH) FIRST CHAMPIONSHIP

Aug	26	(h)	Stoke City	W	4-0	Parkes 2, Iverson, Edwards	25,000
Sep	2	(a)	Stoke City	L	1-3	Parkes	10,000
	9	(a)	Wolves	W	2-1	Haycock, Iverson	14,000
	16	(h)	Wolves	W	3-1	Parkes, Iverson, Haycock	18,000
	23	(h)	Walsall	D	1-1	Edwards	16,000
	30	(a)	Walsall	W	2-0	Broome, Haycock	10,000
Oct	7	(a)	Birmingham	L	2-3	Broome, Houghton	22,000
	14	(h)	Birmingham	D	1-1	Houghton	25,000
	21	(h)	W.B.A.	D	2-2	Parkes, Iverson	25,200
	28	(a)	W.B.A.	W	5-1	Parkes, Iverson, Houghton, Millard (og), Haycock	25,478
Nov	4	(a)	Port Vale	L	1-2	Iverson	9,500
	11	(h)	Port Vale	W	4-0	Houghton, Griffiths (og), Edwards, Haycock	4,400
	18	(h)	Coventry C	W	4-0	Edwards 2, Goffin, Houghton	15,000
	25	(a)	Coventry C	W	6-0	Goffin, Haycock 2, Massie, Edwards, Houghton	10,450
Dec	2	(a)	Leicester C	W	3-0	Edwards, Houghton 2	10,000
	9	(h)	Leicester C	W	5-0	Goffin, Houghton 3, Haycock	12,000
	16	(h)	Northampton T	W	5-2	Houghton 2, Iverson, Edwards 2	9,000
	23	(a)	Northampton T	W	3-2	Shepherson (og), Goffin 2	6,000

FOOTBALL LEAGUE (NORTH) SECOND CHAMPIONSHIP

Dec	26	(h)	W.B.A.*	L	3-4	Parkes 2, Iverson	5,007
	30	(a)	Northampton T	L	0-2		5,000
Jan	6	(a)	W.B.A.	W	3-1	Massie, Iverson, Edwards	21,995
	13	(h)	W.B.A.	W	6-2	Iverson, Houghton, Haycock 2, Edwards 2	15,000
	20	(h)	Birmingham	W	3-1	Edwards, Houghton, Iverson	17,000
	27	(a)	Birmingham	W	1-0	Edwards	16,000
Feb	3	(a)	Coventry C	W	3-2	Goffin, Edwards, Houghton	7,000
	10	(h)	Coventry C	W	5-2	Edwards 2, Broome, Iverson 2	19,000
	17	(h)	Walsall	W	6-1	Houghton 2, Edwards 2, Broome, Iverson	10,000
	24	(a)	Walsall	W	2-0	Iverson, Edwards	10,000
Mar	3	(h)	Northampton T	D	2-2	Houghton 2 (1 pen)	21,000
	10	(h)	Birmingham	W	5-0	Iverson 2, Edwards 2, Houghton	20,000
	17	(a)	Birmingham	W	3-0	Edwards, Iverson, Houghton	19,000
	24	(h)	Wolves	L	1-2	Houghton	32,000
	31	(a)	Wolves	L	0-1		39,000
Apr	2	(a)	W.B.A.	W	4-2	Edwards 3, Iverson	14,378
	7	(a)	Leicester C	L	0-2		7,000
	14	(h)	Leicester C	W	7-2	Edwards 2, Goffin, Houghton 3, Parkes	7,500
	21	(a)	Stoke City	L	0-1		6,000
	28	(h)	Stoke City	W	2-0	Edwards, Goffin	15,000
May	5	(h)	Coventry C	W	9-2	Iverson, Parkes, Goffin, Houghton, Edwards 4, Massie	7,500
	12	(a)	Coventry C	L	1-3	Iverson	5,130
	19	(h)	Derby County	L	0-3		30,000
	21	(h)	Wolves	D	4-4	Iverson, Broome 2, Houghton	7,000
	26	(a)	Derby County	L	0-6		16,218

Freddie Haycock

Appearances (League & Cup): F.H. Broome 20, E. Callaghan 38, L. Canning 1, G. Cummings 40, G.R. Edwards 37, L.L. Godfrey 4, W.C. Goffin 18, R. Guttridge 9, F. Haycock 34, W.E. Houghton 43, R.T. Iverson 36, L. Latham 1, J. Martin 1, A. Massie 34, J.E. McConnon 2, J.H. Morby 3, H. Parkes 26, V.E. Potts 41*, R.W. Starling 42, A. Wakeman 43 — **Total 473.** * *Guest player.*

Goalscorers (L & C): Edwards 33, Houghton 28, Iverson 21, Haycock 10, Parkes 10, Griffin 9, Broome 7, Massie 3, opponents 3 — **Total 124.**

RECORD

P	W	D	L	F	A
43	26	5	12	124	64

* Match was abandoned after 81 minutes due to fog but the result was allowed to stand.
Matches v Coventry and Derby County during May were the semi-final and two legged final ties of the Cup competition.

Aston Villa

Season 1945-46

FOOTBALL LEAGUE SOUTH

Aug	25	(a)	Luton T	D	1-1	Edwards	12,000
	29	(a)	W.B.A.	L	0-1		15,898
Sep	1	(h)	Luton T	W	7-1	Broome 2, Gager (og), Edwards 4	25,000
	5	(h)	W.B.A.	D	3-3	Edwards, Parkes, Goffin	36,103
	8	(h)	Swansea T	W	6-3	Iverson 2, Goffin, Kerr 2, Edwards	25,500
	10	(a)	West Ham	W	2-1	Edwards, Martin	23,000
	15	(a)	Swansea T	L	4-5	Goffin, Iverson 2, Kerr	15,000
	22	(a)	Arsenal	W	4-2	Iverson 2, Edwards, Kerr	35,000
	29	(h)	Arsenal	W	5-1	Edwards 4, Broome	50,000
Oct	6	(a)	Charlton A	D	0-0		50,000
	13	(h)	Charlton A	L	0-2		48,000
	20	(h)	Fulham	W	3-0	Edwards, Broome, Iverson	15,000
	27	(a)	Fulham	W	4-0	Edwards 2, Iverson 2	34,500
Nov	3	(a)	Plymouth A	W	3-0	Edwards 3	33,038
	10	(h)	Plymouth A	W	4-2	Martin 2, Iverson, Edwards	25,000
	17	(h)	Portsmouth	W	3-2	Iverson, Guthrie (og), Edwards	20,000
	24	(a)	Portsmouth	W	3-2	Edwards 2, Martin	30,000
Dec	1	(h)	Nottm Forest	W	3-1	Parkes, Smith, Edwards	30,000
	8	(a)	Nottm Forest	W	3-1	Martin, Edwards 2	30,224
	19	(h)	Newport C	W	5-2	Graham, Broome 2, Parkes, Edwards	20,000
	22	(a)	Newport C	W	4-0	Iverson, Martin, Smith, Edwards	17,500
	25	(a)	Wolves	W	2-1	Iverson, Edwards	30,000
	28	(h)	Wolves	D	1-1	Martin	59,970
	29	(h)	West Ham	D	2-2	Martin, Iverson	34,000
Jan	12	(h)	Birmingham	D	2-2	Jennings (og), Edwards	63,820
	19	(a)	Birmingham	L	1-3	Edwards	40,000
Feb	2	(h)	Tottenham	W	5-1	Edwards 2, Broome 2, Cummings	25,000
	26	(a)	Brentford	W	1-0	Iverson	27,000
	20	(a)	Tottenham	L	0-3		18,500
	23	(a)	Chelsea	D	2-2	Goffin, Iverson	45,000
Mar	16	(a)	Millwall	D	2-2	Soo (og), Broome	11,000
	23	(a)	Southampton	W	5-3	Edwards 2, Goffin, Broome 2	23,000
	27	(h)	Chelsea	L	0-3		18,000
	30	(h)	Southampton	W	2-0	Smith, Edwards	25,000
Apr	6	(h)	Derby C	W	4-1	Broome 2, Edwards, Dixon	49,875
	13	(a)	Derby C	W	1-0	Dixon	30,000
	17	(h)	Brentford	D	1-1	Broome	18,000
	20	(h)	Coventry C	D	0-0		40,000
	22	(h)	Leicester C	W	3-0	Dixon, Goffin 2	30,000
	23	(a)	Leicester C	W	1-0	Martin	20,000
	27	(a)	Coventry C	D	2-2	Edwards, Houghton (pen)	12,000
May	1	(h)	Millwall	W	2-0	Houghton (pen), Edwards	31,000

TOP WARTIME APPEARANCES

V.E. Potts	204
A. Wakeman	192
G. Cummings	188
R.T. Iverson	181
W.E. Houghton	159
E. Callaghan	155
R.W. Starling	147
H. Parkes	146
F.H. Broome	142
A. Massie	133
G.R. Edwards	131
W.C. Goffin	86
F. Haycock	85
J.R. Martin	54

TOP WARTIME GOALSCORERS

G.R. Edwards	98
F.H. Broome	96
W.E. Houghton	89
R.D. Davis	67
R.T. Iverson	56
W.C. Goffin	51
H. Parkes	41
F. Haycock	25
A.W. Kerr	21
J.R. Martin	16

FA CUP

Jan	5	(a)	Coventry C	L	1-2	Smith	27,000
	8	(h)	Coventry C	W	2-0	Smith, Goffin	20,000
	26	(a)	Millwall	W	4-2	Goffin, Edwards 2, Smith	30,000
	28	(h)	Millwall	W	9-1	Goffin 2, Parkes, Broome 3, Edwards, Smith, Iverson	28,000
Feb	9	(a)	Chelsea	W	1-0	Broome	60,000
	12	(h)	Chelsea	W	1-0	Goffin	56,000
Mar	2	(h)	Derby C	L	3-4	Edwards, Iverson, Broome	76,558
	9	(a)	Derby C	D	1-1	Broome	31,000

Appearances (League & Cup): R.M. Beresford 1, F.H. Broome 33, G. Cummings 50, E. Callaghan 30, W.J. Carry 1, J.T. Dixon 5, G.R. Edwards 43, L.L. Godfrey 3, W.C. Goffin 24, J. Graham 4, F. Haycock 1, W.E. Houghton 14, R.T. Iverson 49, A.W. Kerr 11, E. Love 32, A. Massie 3, J.R. Martin 26, J.H. Morby 12, F. Moss 12, H.A. Parkes 38, V.E. Potts 47, J. Rutherford 9, F.H. Shell 4, R.A. Scott 2*, L.G.F. Smith 30, R.W. Starling 28, A. Wakeman 38 — **Total 550.** * *Guest player.*

Goalscorers (L & C): Edwards 43, Broome 20, Iverson 18, Goffin 12, Martin 9, Smith 7, Kerr 4, Parkes 4, opponents 4, Dixon 3, Houghton 2, Cummings 1, Graham 1 — **Total 128.**

RECORD

	P	W	D	L	F	A	Post
F/L/S	42	25	11	6	106	57	2nd
FAC	8	5	1	2	22	10	Rd 6
Total	50	30	12	8	128	67	—

Aston Villa's first team squad in 1945-46.
Back row (left to right): 'Mush' Callaghan, Harry Parkes, Eddie Lowe, Alan Wakeman, George Edwards, Jack Morby.
Front row: Billy Goffin, Frank Broome, George Cummings, Les Smith, Vic Potts and Bob Iverson.

Villa's complete Wartime Record

Season	P	W	D	L	F	A
1939-40	3	1	0	2	3	3
1940-41	20	5	1	14	50	57
1941-42	29	24	1	4	135	27
1942-43	38	23	3	12	91	63
1943-44	40	24	7	9	94	62
1944-45	43	26	5	12	124	64
1945-46 (L)	42	25	11	6	106	57
(FAC)	8	5	1	2	22	10
Totals	223	133	29	61	625	343

Birmingham

Season 1939-40

FOOTBALL LEAGUE DIVISION 2

Aug	26	(a)	Tottenham	D	1-1	Brown	28,366
	30	(h)	Leicester C	W	2-0	Farrage, Sharman (og)	15,000
Sep	2	(h)	Burnley	W	2-0	Dearson, Duckhouse	20,000

MIDLAND REGIONAL LEAGUE

Oct	21	(a)	Wolves	W	3-2	Broome, Edwards, Dearson	6,428
	28	(a)	Walsall	W	2-1	Jennings, Dearson	4,554
Nov	4	(a)	Luton Town	W	2-1	Duckhouse, Dearson	4,000
	11	(a)	Coventry C	L	1-3	Brown	5,501
	18	(a)	W.B.A.	D	2-2	Brown 2	8,671
	25	(a)	Leicester C	W	3-1	Jones, Bye, Edwards	4,104
Dec	2	(a)	Northampton T	D	1-1	Jones	4,088
	9	(a)	Wolves	L	2-6	Broome 2	2,705
	16	(a)	Walsall	W	2-1	Edwards, Broome	2,464
	27	(a)	W.B.A.	L	0-3		7,000
	30	(n*)	Coventry C	L	2-4	Broome, Bodle	2,900
Jan	13	(n*)	Leicester C	D	3-3	Guest 2, Duckhouse	2,000
	20	(a)	Northampton T	L	0-3		1,500
Feb	10	(a)	Luton T	L	2-4	Harris (pen), Roberts (og)	3,026
	24	(a)	W.B.A.	L	1-6	Edwards	6,799
Mar	2	(a)	Leicester C	L	1-2	Jones	2,140
	9	(a)	Northampton T	W	3-1	Turner (pen), Brown, Bodle	3,117
	16	(a)	Wolves	L	1-3	Bodle	4,351
	23	(h)	Walsall	W	2-1	Jones 2	13,241
	25	(a)	W.B.A.	L	1-4	Duckhouse	9,986
	26	(h)	Luton Town	W	5-4	Bodle 2, Jones 2, Godden	10,052
	30	(h)	Luton Town	W	4-1	Jones, Trigg 2, Bodle	7,000
Apr	6	(h)	Coventry C	W	2-0	Trigg 2	8,138
	10	(h)	Wolves	L	0-1		7,227
	20	(a)	Newport C.	D	2-2	Godden 2	4,000
	27	(h)	Newport C.	W	5-2	Trigg 2, Bodle 2, Godden	6,992
May	1	(h)	Northampton T	W	3-1	Gardner, Bodle, Trigg	4,076
	4	(h)	Reading	W	2-0	Trigg, Jones	9,567
	11	(a)	Reading	W	2-0	Godden, Bodle	4,827
	18	(n§)	Arsenal	W	2-1	Trigg, Turner	11,259
	20	(n)	Leicester C	D	0-0		1,500
	25	(a)	West Ham U	L	2-4	Trigg 2	18,500
Jun	5	(h)	Coventry C	D	0-0		1,000
	8	(h)	Walsall	W	8-1	Bodle 2, Duckhouse 2, Jones 2, Brown, Godfrey (og)	1,000

* Played at Leamington. § Played at White Hart Lane, London. Matches v Newport (h & a), Reading (h & a), Arsenal and West Ham during April and May were all in the League Cup competition.

Appearances (League & Cup): J.P. Allen 1*, J. Bate 1*, S.C. Bellamy 4, H. Bodle 23, F.H. Broome 7*, E. Brown 1, J. Brown 23, J.H. Bye 26, C. Craven 9, G. Cummings 4*, F.A. Deakin 4*, D.J. Dearson 27, R. Devey 3*, E. Duckhouse 9, G.R. Edwards 10*, T.O. Farrage 3, R.E. Foulkes 7, F.C. Gardner 2, A.E. Godden 11, F. Guest 6*, F. Harris 28, H.E. Hibbs 12, W.M. Hughes 26, R.T. Iverson 7*, D.B. Jennings 8, C.W. Jones 20, D.H.G. Kernick 1*, J.R. Martin 2*, A. Massie 4*, G.H. Merrick 1, S. Morris 1, F. Moss 2*, F.W. Moss 1, W. Quinton 24, S. Rowley 1, R. Shaw 13, C. Trigg 25, A. Turner 26, W.J. Wheeler 24 — **Total 407.** * *Guest player.*

Goalscorers (L & C): Bodle 12, Jones 11, Trigg 11, J. Brown 6, Duckhouse 6, Broome 5, Godden 5, Dearson 4, Edwards 4, Guest 2, Turner 2, Bye 1, Farrage 1, Gardner 1, Harris 1, Jennings 1, opponents own-goals 3 — **Total 76.**

RECORD

P	W	D	L	F	A
37	18	7	12	76	76

Season 1940-41

FOOTBALL LEAGUE (SOUTH)

Aug	31	(a)	Nottingham F	W	3-2	Jones, Bodle Goddle	1,500
Sep	7	(h)	Nottingham F	W	2-1	Trigg, Bye	3,600
	14	(a)	Cardiff C	L	2-5	Trigg 2	3,000
	21	(h)	Cardiff C	W	3-2	Harris (pen), Trigg 2	3,064
	28	(a)	W.B.A.	W	2-1	Dearson, Eastham	4,718
Oct	5	(h)	W.B.A.	L	1-3	Jones	5,394
	12	(a)	Mansfield T	L	1-4	Jennings	2,000
	19	(h)	Mansfield T	W	4-1	Trigg 2, Jones, Harris (pen)	1,200
	26	(a)	Leicester C	L	1-2	Gardner	3,000
Nov	2	(h)	Leicester C	L	1-2	Trigg	500
	9	(a)	Stoke City	L	0-5		4,980
	16	(h)	Stoke City	W	6-2	Trigg 5, Craven	1,462
	30	(a)	Notts County	D	3-3	Trigg 3	600
Dec	7	(a)	Northampton T	L	1-2	Trigg	2,000
	25	(a)	Walsall	L	3-6	Trigg 3	2,891
Feb	15	(a)	Leicester C	D	3-3	Dearson, Shaw, Gardner	3,917
	22	(a)	Leicester C	L	2-3	Gardner, Dearson	4,500
Mar	1	(a)	Luton Town	W	5-2	Dearson 3, Gill, Forsyth (og)	4,500

Matches v Leicester in February were League War Cup games.

Appearances (League & Cup): S.G. Batty 1*, H. Bodle 1, J. Brown 7, J.H. Bye 6, C. Craven 4, F.A. Deakin 7, D.J. Dearson 14, R. Devey 4, G.R. Eastham 6*, R.E. Foulkes 14, D.S. Galley 1, F.C. Gardner 12, J. Gill 5*, A.E. Godden 6, F. Harris 13, W.M. Hughes 12, D.B. Jennings 12, C.W. Jones 12, D.H.G. Kernick 4*, G.H. Merrick 13, S. Morris 1, F.W. Moss 1, H. Pearce 2, W. Quinton 16, R. Shaw 3, W. Thayne 1*, C. Trigg 12, A. Turner 3, W.J. Wheeler 5 — **Total 198.** * *Guest player.*

Goalscorers (L & C): Trigg 20, Dearson 6, Gardner 3, Jones 3, Harris 2, Bye 1, Bodle 1, Eastham 1, Craven 1, Godden 1, Gill 1, Jennings 1, Shaw 1, opponent own-goal 1 — **Total 43.**

RECORD

P	W	D	L	F	A
18	7	2	9	43	49

Birmingham did not compete in any major competition in season 1941-42.

Ray Devey

Birmingham

Season 1942-43

FOOTBALL LEAGUE NORTH (1st COMPETITION)

Aug	29	(a)	Leciester C	W	1-0	McCormick	4,000
Sep	5	(h)	Leicester C	W	2-1	Brown, Shaw	7,000
	12	(h)	Derby C	L	0-5		6,000
	19	(a)	Derby C	L	1-3	Ottewell	10,000
	26	(a)	Northampton T	L	1-4	Ottewell	3,000
Oct	3	(h)	Northampton T	L	0-2		5,000
	10	(h)	Stoke City	W	1-0	Acquaroff	2,500
	17	(a)	Stoke City	W	3-1	Bate, Craven, Gill	4,000
	24	(a)	Coventry C	D	2-2	Acquaroff 2	8,638
	31	(h)	Coventry C	W	1-0	Harris	5,000
Nov	7	(h)	Walsall	W	4-3	Watton, Dearson 3	4,000
	14	(a)	Walsall	L	0-1		2,500
	21	(a)	Aston Villa	L	1-2	Cummings (og)	15,000
	28	(h)	Aston Villa	W	2-1	Callaghan (og), Watton	15,000
Dec	5	(h)	W.B.A.	W	3-0	Dearson, Ottewell 2	3,000
	12	(a)	W.B.A.	L	3-4	McCormick 2, Craven	3,393
	19	(a)	Wolves	D	1-1	Jones	1,200
	25	(a)	Wolves	W	1-0	Jones	2,000
	26	(a)	Northampton T	L	1-5	McCormick	7,000
Jan	2	(h)	Northampton T	L	2-4	Dearson, Jones	2,000
	9	(h)	Leicester C	W	5-0	McCormick, Howe (og), Jones 2, Craven	1,000
	16	(a)	Leicester C	L	1-2	Acquaroff	5,000
	23	(a)	Walsall	D	1-1	Jones	3,000
	30	(h)	Walsall	W	1-0	Acquaroff	1,000
Feb	6	(h)	W.B.A.	L	0-1		8,000
	13	(a)	W.B.A.	L	1-2	McEwan	7,217
	20	(a)	Coventry C	L	0-1		7,578
	27	(h)	Coventry C	W	3-1	Craven, Watton, McEwan	2,000
Mar	6	(a)	Walsall	W	2-1	Watton, Trickett	1,500
	13	(h)	Walsall	W	2-1	Romp, Turner	700
	20	(h)	Coventry C	L	1-2	Acquaroff	1,000
	27	(a)	Coventry C	L	1-2	Acquaroff	4,864
Apr	3	(h)	W.B.A.	W	5-3	Ottewell 3, Watton, Dearson	4,000
	10	(a)	W.B.A.	W	4-0	Craven, Dearson, Lewis, Richards	1,818
	17	(h)	Northampton T	W	1-0	Eden	1,900
	24	(a)	Northampton T	L	0-1		2,000
	26	(a)	Aston Villa	L	0-1		5,000
May	1	(a)	Chesterfield	D	1-1	Acquaroff	1,800

Appearances (League & Cup): J. Acquaroff 31*, G.E. Ainsley 1*, S. Bartram 1*, J. Bate 1*, S.G. Batty 2*, S.C. Bellamy 1, H. Bodle 1, J. Bray 1*, J. Brown 3, D.J. Buttens 1, J.H. Bye 3, S. Chapman 1*, G.E. Collins 2*, J.F. Collins 2, C. Craven 24, H. Davy 4, F.A. Deakin 1, D.J. Dearson 23, R. Devey 2, L.G. Dolphin 2, E. Eden 7, R.J. Finian 1*, R. Ford 1, J.D. Gill 7, W.D. Goffin 1*, W.F. Guest 2*, E.A. Hapgood 1*, G.F.M. Hardwick 1*, F. Harris 4, W.M. Hughes 1, P.J. Jenkins 1, D.B. Jennings 37, C.W. Jones 6, S.H. King 1, C.J. Lewis 6, J. McCormick 28*, W. McEwan 3*, G.H. Merrick 35, N. Middleton 2, E. Millichap 2, F. Mitchell 16*, F.W. Moss 1, S. Ottewell 13*, W.T. Pears 2, T.U. Pearson 2*, J. Pope 1, W. Quinton 30, E. Richards 3, G.H. Robinson 2*, L.W. Romp 1, J. Shaw 1, R. Shaw 31, J.B.T. Shelton 1*, E. Sibley 1*, T.W. Smith 1, F. Sweeney 1, G. Tranter 2, J.E. Trickett 1, C. Trigg 5, A. Turner 32, P.G. Vause 1*, G.D. Watton 14, F. Watts 1, W. Webber 1* — **Total 418.** * *Guest player.*

Goalscorers (L & C): Acquaroff 8, Dearson 7, Ottewell 7, Jones 6, Craven 5, McCormick 5, Watton 5, McEwan 2, Bate 1, Brown 1, Eden 1, Gill 1, Harris 1, Lewis 1, Richards 1, Romp 1, R. Shaw 1, Trickett 1, Turner 1, opponent own-goals 3 — **Total 59.**

RECORD

P	W	D	L	F	A
38	17	4	17	59	59

Season 1943-44

FOOTBALL LEAGUE NORTH

Aug	28	(a)	Coventry C	D	0-0		7,000
Sep	4	(h)	Coventry C	L	1-2	Revell	7,929
	11	(h)	Leicester C	W	3-0	Hinsley 2 (1 pen), Acquaroff	6,000
	18	(a)	Leicester C	D	2-2	Hinsley, Bright	3,500
	25	(h)	Northampton T	L	1-3	Gee	4,000
Oct	2	(a)	Northampton T	L	1-2	Shaw	4,000
	9	(a)	Derby County	L	3-5	Mulraney, Trigg 2	8,000
	16	(h)	Derby County	D	3-3	Trigg, Bright, Bye	4,500
	23	(a)	Stoke City	D	1-1	Dearson	5,000
	30	(h)	Stoke City	W	2-0	Trigg, Mulraney	3,900
Nov	6	(a)	Walsall	W	4-2	Trigg 2, Bright, Dearson	3,500
	13	(h)	Walsall	W	5-1	Trigg 2 (1 pen), Mulraney 2, Bright	3,000
	20	(h)	Aston Villa	W	2-1	Mulraney, Dearson	20,000
	27	(a)	Aston Villa	L	0-3		15,000
Dec	4	(a)	W.B.A.	W	3-1	Mulraney 2, Trigg	5,494
	11	(h)	W.B.A.	W	3-0	Roberts, Trigg 2 (1 pen)	5,156
	18	(h)	Wolves	W	4-2	Trigg 2, Doherty, Bright	4,000
	25	(a)	Wolves	L	0-3		7,000
	26	(a)	W.B.A.	D	1-1	Shaw	14,717
Jan	1	(h)	W.B.A.	W	4-0	Bright 2, Trigg, Mulraney	9,142
	8	(h)	Northampton T	W	5-1	Trigg, Roberts, Mulraney 2, Dearson	1,500
	22	(h)	Stoke City	W	4-1	Mitchell, Acquaroff, Mulraney, Bright	1,750
	29	(a)	Stoke City	L	1-4	Trigg	20,000
Feb	5	(a)	Wolves	W	2-0	Trigg 2	7,000
	12	(h)	Wolves	W	2-1	Trigg (pen), Bright	8,000
	19	(h)	Aston Villa	D	1-1	Trigg	18,000
	26	(a)	Aston Villa	W	2-1	Trigg 2	21,000
Mar	4	(h)	Leicester C	W	3-1	Mulraney, Trigg 2	12,000
	11	(a)	Leicester C	L	1-2*	Bright	15,000
	18	(h)	Manchester U	W	3-1	Bodle, Shaw, Trigg	16,000
	25	(a§)	Manchester U	D	1-1	Trigg	32,992
Apr	1	(a)	Manchester C	L	0-1		27,173
	8	(h)	Manchester C	D	0-0		39,552
	10	(a)	Coventry C	W	3-0	Trigg 2, Godden	5,860
	15	(a)	Walsall	D	2-2	Trigg 2	2,000
	22	(h)	Walsall	W	5-0	Jennings, Trigg 4	4,000
	29	(h)	Northampton T	W	3-1	Morris, Trigg (pen), Dearson	6,000
May	6	(a)	Northampton T	W	5-0	Roberts 2, Mulraney 2, Faulkner	1,850

* After extra-time. §Played at Maine Road, Manchester. Matches from 26th December to 26th February inclusive were League North Cup Qualifying games, and matches from 4th March to 8th April inclusive were in the League North Cup proper.

Appearances (League & Cup): J. Acquaroff 13*, R.H. Barnett 4, H. Bodle 4, R.L. Bright 27*, J.H. Bye 4, C. Craven 6, E.F. Day 1, D.J. Dearson 30, P.D. Doherty 4*, L.G. Dolphin 1, R. Faulkner 1*, H. Gee 2, A.E. Godden 2, K. Green 7, J. Hackett 1, F. Harris 4, L.E. Hayward 2*, G. Hinsley 5*, W.M. Hughes 5, D.B. Jennings 26, W.V.A. Jones 1, T. McKillop 1*, G.H. Merrick 38, N. Middleton 2, F.R. Mitchell 11, J.D. Montgomery 1, L.D. Morgan 1*, S. Morris 2, A. Mulraney 33*, S. Ottewell 1*, T. Peacock 1*, W. Quinton 24, H. Redwood 1*, C. Revell 1*, N.E. Roberts 2, T.D. Roberts 16, R. Shaw 32, T. Sibley 2, M. Sinclair 1*, S.H. Stanton 7, T. Stanton 1, J.E. Trickett 1, D. Trigg 30, A. Turner 32, H. Turner 27* — **Total 418.** * *Guest player.*

Goalscorers (L & C): Trigg 35, Bright 10, T. Roberts 4, Shaw 3, Bodle 1, Faulkner 1, Godden 1, Mitchell 1, Revell 1, Mulraney 14, Dearson 5, Hinsley 3, Acquaroff 2, Bye 1, Gee 1, Jennings 1, Morris 1, Doherty 1 — **Total 86.**

RECORD

P	W	D	L	F	A
38	20	9	9	86	50

Birmingham

Season 1944-45

FOOTBALL LEAGUE NORTH

Aug	26	(a)	Port Vale	L	0-3		7,000
Sep	2	(h)	Port Vale	W	4-0	Trigg 4	12,000
	9	(h)	Coventry C	L	1-2	Craven	10,000
	16	(a)	Coventry C	W	1-0	Faulkner	9,927
	23	(a)	Leicester C	W	1-0	Shaw	7,000
	30	(h)	Leicester C	D	3-3	Mulraney 2, Trigg	10,000
Oct	7	(h)	Aston Villa	W	3-2	Mulraney, Trigg 2	22,000
	14	(a)	Aston Villa	D	1-1	Bright	25,000
	21	(a)	Stoke City	D	0-0		6,000
	28	(h)	Stoke City	D	1-1	Bright	8,000
Nov	4	(h)	Wolves	W	1-0	Small	12,000
	11	(a)	Wolves	W	4-0	Trigg 3, Faulkner	8,000
	18	(a)	Walsall	L	1-4	Small	4,500
	25	(h)	Walsall	D	2-2	Mulligan (og), Shelton (og)	5,000
Dec	2	(h)	Northampton T	D	0-0		9,000
	9	(a)	Northampton T	L	1-2	Small	3,000
	16	(h)	W.B.A.	W	2-0	Tranter (og), Trigg	6,796
	23	(a)	W.B.A.	W	4-1	Trigg 2, White 2	5,000
	26	(h)	Wolves	D	0-0		6,000
	30	(h)	Walsall	W	3-1	Trigg 3	10,000
Jan	6	(h)	Coventry C	W	5-1	Hikins, Trigg 3, White	12,000
	13	(a)	Coventry C	W	2-1	White, Trigg	5,084
	20	(a)	Aston Villa	L	1-3	Harris	17,000
	27	(h)	Aston Villa	L	0-1		16,000
Feb	3	(h)	Northampton T	W	4-0	Bodle 2, Trigg 2	2,000
	10	(a)	Northampton T	L	1-2	Mulraney	5,000
	17	(a)	W.B.A.	L	0-4		12,479
	24	(h)	W.B.A.	D	1-1	Dearson	17,727
Mar	3	(a)	Walsall	W	2-0	Kernick 2	4,000
	10	(a)	Aston Villa	L	0-5		20,000
	17	(h)	Aston Villa	L	0-3		19,000
	24	(a)	Northampton T	W	2-0	Mulraney, Massart	8,000
	31	(h)	Northampton T	D	2-2	Massart, Mulraney	18,000
Apr	2	(a)	Wolves	L	1-2	Turner (pen)	12,000
	7	(h)	Wolves	D	0-0		27,000
	14	(a)	Wolves	L	0-1*		25,000
May	5	(h)	W.B.A.	W	4-1	Massart 3, Lewis	1,025
	12	(a)	W.B.A.	W	3-2	Massart 3	10,947
	19	(h)	Nottingham F	W	4-1	Mulraney, Massart, Dearson, Matthews	3,000
	26	(a)	Nottingham F	D	0-0		2,900

MIDLAND LEAGUE CUP

Apr	21	(h)	Coventry C	L	1-2	Bright	8,015
	28	(a)	Coventry C	D	2-2	Lewis, Bright	3,867

* After extra-time. Matches from 30th December to 3rd March inclusive were League North Cup Qualifying games, and matches played on 24th and 31st March and 7th and 14th April were in the League Cup North proper.

Appearances (League & Cup): H.S. Adams 1, R.T. Ball 1, R.H. Barnett 1, J.R. Berry 2, H. Bodle 4, W.S. Booth 6*, R.L. Bright 19*, A.B. Clements 1, C. Craven 12, D.J. Dearson 38, J.M. Elliott 1, K.G. Faulkner 14, J.W. Fenton 1, A.A. Garrett 1*, J. Greatrix 1, F. Harris 6, W. Harris 1, W.A. Hicklin 11, D. Hikins 10, W.M. Hughes 7, N. Jenks 2, D.B. Jennings 40, C. Jordan 1*, D.H.G. Kernick 3*, S.H. King 3, S.G. King 3, R. Lewes 3, A.H.P. Marriott 4, G.B.H. Martin 1, D.L. Massart 9, J.B. Matthews 2, G.H. Merrick 38, W.F. Metcalf 5*, F.R. Mitchell 7, F. Micheson 1*, S. Morris 3, A. Mulraney 37, R.E. Murrell 2, H. O'Donnell 3*, A.L. Pope 1*, W. Quinton 12, T.D. Roberts 2, R. Shaw 30, T. Sibley 2, S.J. Small 24*, S.R. Smith 1, S. Stanton 14, D.H. Trentham 1*, C. Trigg 22, A. Turner 39, H. Turner 1*, F.R.H. White 10*, I. Williams 1 — **Total 462.** * *Guest player.*

Goalscorers (L & C): Trigg 22, Massart 9, Mulraney 7, Bright 4, White 4, Small 3, Bodle 2, Dearson 2, Faulkner 2, Lewis 2, Kernick 2, Craven 1, Harris 1, Hikins 1, Matthews 1, Shaw 1, Turner 1, opponents own-goals 3 — **Total 68.**

RECORD

P	W	D	L	F	A
42	17	12	13	68	56

Ambrose 'Jock' Mulraney

Gil Merrick

Birmingham

Season 1945-46

FOOTBALL LEAGUE SOUTH

Aug	25	(h)	West Ham U	L 0-1		30,000
Sep	1	(a)	West Ham U	L 2-3	Massart, Edwards	20,000
	3	(h)	Luton Town	W 3-2	Dougall 2, Bodle	12,000
	8	(h)	W.B.A.	W 4-0	Edwards, Mulraney, Duckhouse, Jones	20,068
	15	(a)	W.B.A.	D 0-0		27,745
	17	(a)	Coventry C	W 3-2	Bodle, Duckhouse, Mulraney	14,416
	22	(a)	Swansea T	W 4-2	Mulraney, Dougall, Massart 2	18,000
	29	(h)	Swansea T	W 5-0	Bodle 2, Duckhouse, Jones, Mulraney	14,000
Oct	6	(h)	Tottenham H	W 8-0	Duckhouse, Massart 2, Dougall, Bodle, Edwards, Mulraney 2	21,608
	13	(a)	Tottenham H	W 1-0	Mulraney	30,589
	20	(a)	Brentford	L 1-2	White	20,690
	27	(h)	Brentford	W 1-0	Massart	34,788
Nov	3	(h)	Chelsea	W 5-2	Bodle 2, Jones, Turner (pen), Edwards	26,858
	10	(a)	Chelsea	W 3-2	Jones 2, Turner (pen)	53,813
	17	(a)	Millwall	L 1-5	Jones	17,500
	24	(h)	Millwall	W 4-0	Bodle, Jones, Edwards 2	20,000
Dec	1	(a)	Southampton	D 1-1	Duckhouse	18,000
	8	(h)	Southampton	W 4-0	Bodle 2, Duckhouse, Edwards	20,000
	15	(a)	Derby County	W 2-0	Edwards, Jones	20,000
	22	(h)	Derby County	W 1-0	Bodle	30,000
	25	(h)	Leicester C	W 6-2	Jones 2, Dougall, Bodle, Edwards, Mulraney	30,000
	26	(a)	Leicester C	W 1-0	Mulraney	24,460
	29	(h)	Coventry C	W 2-0	Edwards, Dougall	24,107
Jan	12	(a)	Aston Villa	D 2-2	Dearson, Dougall	63,820
	19	(h)	Aston Villa	W 3-1	Jones 2, Mulraney	40,000
Feb	2	(a)	Arsenal	W 3-0	Jones, Edwards 2	30,416
	16	(h)	Charlton A	W 1-0	Jones	56,615
	23	(h)	Fulham	W 2-0	Laing, White	25,000
Mar	13	(h)	Arsenal	L 0-1		14,683
	16	(h)	Plymouth A	L 0-1		21,884
	30	(a)	Portsmouth	W 4-3	Mulraney, Jones, Dougall, Bodle	24,389
Apr	1	(a)	Plymouth A	W 3-2	Jones 3	10,000
	6	(a)	Nottingham F	L 0-1		24,289
	10	(h)	Portsmouth	W 1-0	Jones	14,920
	13	(h)	Nottingham F	W 3-1	Bodle, Jones, Harris	28,000
	15	(a)	Fulham	L 2-3	Dougall 2	14,000
	19	(h)	Newport C	W 3-2	Mulraney, Massart 2	19,790
	20	(a)	Wolves	D 3-3	Bodle, Edwards, Harris	42,684
	22	(a)	Newport C	W 1-0	Massart	14,220
	27	(h)	Wolves	L 0-1		25,000
	29	(a)	Charlton A	D 0-0		30,000
May	4	(a)	Luton Town	W 3-0	Bodle, Mitchell (pen), Mulraney	15,854

FINAL LEAGUE POSITION: 1st in Football League South.

Charlie Wilson Jones

F.A. CUP

Jan	5	(h)	Portsmouth	W 1-0	Flewin (og)	33,845
	9	(a)	Portsmouth	D 0-0		23,716
	26	(h)	Watford	W 5-0	Mulraney 3, Jones, Bodle	25,000
	30	(a)	Watford	D 1-1	Jones	6,000
Feb	9	(a)	Sunderland	L 0-1		45,000
	13	(h)	Sunderland	W 3-1	Jones 2, Mulraney	40,000
Mar	2	(a)	Bradford	D 2-2	Dougall, Jones	19,732
	9	(h)	Bradford	W 6-0	Dougall 2, Bodle 2, Mulraney 2	46,858
	23	(n§)	Derby C SF	D 1-1	Mulraney	65,013
	27	(n+)	Derby C R	L 0-4*		80,480

§ Played at Hillsborough, Sheffield. + Played at Maine Road, Manchester. * After extra-time.

Appearances (League): H. Bodle 40, D.J. Dearson 34, E.G. Ditchburn 1*, C. Dougall 38, E. Duckhouse 26, G.R. Edwards 38, F. Harris 39, W.M. Hughes 4, N. Jenks 2, D.B. Jennings 41, C.W. Jones 27, S.H. King 2, R.S. Laing 2, D.L. Massart 11, I. McPherson 1*, G.H. Merrick 39, F.R. Mitchell 26, A. Mulraney 38, S.W. Owen 5, R. Shaw 2, S. Stanton 1, C. Trigg 1, A. Turner 40, F.R.H. White 4* — **Total 462**. * *Guest player.*

Goalscorers (League): Jones 20, Bodle 16, Edwards 13, Mulraney 13, Dougall 10, Massart 9, Duckhouse 6, Harris 2, Turner 2, White 2, Dearson 1, Laing 1, Mitchell 1 — **Total 96.**

F.A. Cup Appearances: H. Bodle 10, C. Dougall 10, E. Duckhouse 10, G.R. Edwards 10, F. Harris 10, D.B. Jennings 10, C.W. Jones 10, S.H. King 2, G.H. Merrick 8, F.R. Mitchell 10, A. Mulraney 10, A. Turner 10 — **Total 110.**

F.A. Cup Goalscorers: Mulraney 7, Jones 5, Bodle 3, Dougall 3, opponent own-goal 1 — **Total 19.**

RECORD

	P	W	D	L	F	A
League (S)	42	28	5	9	96	45
F.A.C.	10	4	4	2	19	10
Total	52	32	9	11	115	55

Birmingham

TOP WARTIME APPEARANCES

A. Turner	186
D. Jennings	174
G. Merrick	172
D. Dearson	166
A. Mulraney	118
R. Shaw	111
F. Harris	104
C. Trigg	95
H. Bodle	83
C.W. Jones	75
F. Mitchell	70
G.R. Edwards	58
W. Hughes	55
R.L. Bright	46
E. Duckhouse	45

TOP WARTIME GOALSCORERS

C. Trigg	88
C.W. Jones	45
A. Mulraney	41
H. Bodle	35
D. Dearson	25
D. Massant	18
G.R. Edwards	17
R.L. Bright	14
N. Dougall	13
J. Acquaroff	10

Birmingham's complete Wartime Record

Season	P	W	D	L	F	A
1939-40	37	18	7	12	76	76
1940-41	18	7	2	9	43	49
1941-42	Did not compete in any competition.					
1942-43	38	17	4	17	59	59
1943-44	38	20	9	9	86	50
1944-45	42	17	12	13	68	56
1945-46 (L)	42	28	5	9	96	45
1945-46 (FAC)	10	4	4	2	19	10
Totals	225	111	43	71	447	345

Blues' keeper Gil Merrick diving at the feet of Derby striker Jack Stamps during the 1945-46 F.A. Cup semi-final at Sheffield.

Arthur Turner — 186 appearances for Blues.

Ted Duckhouse — broke his leg in the semi-final replay v Derby in 1946.

Cyril Trigg

George Edwards

Coventry City

Season 1939-40

FOOTBALL LEAGUE DIVISION 2

Aug	26	(a)	Burnley	D	1-1	Lager	10,000
	28	(h)	W.B.A.	D	3-3	Green 2, Lager	26,000
Sep	2	(h)	Barnsley	W	4-2	Lowrie, Mason, Crawley 2	10,000

REGIONAL LEAGUE MIDLAND DIVISION

Oct	21	(a)	Northampton T	D	1-1	Frith	3,000
	28	(h)	W.B.A.	W	6-3	Green 2, Frith 3, Lowrie	3,056
Nov	4	(a)	Leicester C	L	2-4	Green, Lowrie	3,000
	11	(h)	Birmingham	W	3-1	Frith, Green, Lowrie	5,501
	18	(a)	Wolves	L	0-4		5,210
	25	(h)	Walsall	W	4-3	Lowrie, Crawley 2, Green	2,000
Dec	2	(a)	Luton Town	L	0-7		4,000
	9	(h)	Northampton T	L	1-4	Green	956
	16	(a)	W.B.A.	L	1-3	Lowrie	3,802
	23	(h)	Leicester C	L	0-1		1,212
	30	(a)	Birmingham	W	4-2	Taylor, Green, Crawley 2	2,900
Jan	1	(h)	Wolves	L	0-3		1,879
	13	(a)	Walsall	W	2-0	Taylor, Davidson	1,720
Feb	24	(a)	Wolves	L	0-1		2,532
Mar	2	(h)	Walsall	W	4-1	Crawley 2, Barratt, Davidson	1,528
	9	(a)	Luton Town	W	5-1	Davidson 3, Crawley, Barratt	2,968
	16	(h)	Northampton T	W	6-3	Crawley, Taylor 3, Davidson 2	1,034
	23	(a)	W.B.A.	L	1-3	Crawley	6,743
	25	(h)	Luton Town	W	10-2	Crawley 8, Green, Barratt	5,650
	26	(a)	Northampton T	L	0-2		3,997
	30	(h)	Leicester C	W	4-1	Barratt, Davidson, Green, Crawley	4,036
Apr	6	(a)	Birmingham	L	0-2		8,138
	13	(h)	Wolves	D	1-1	Lauderdale	3,046
May	25	(a)	Walsall	L	1-2	Murray	2,700
	30	(a)	Leicester C	W	3-1	Lauderdale, Murray, Crawley	2,000
June	1	(h)	Luton Town	W	5-1	Lewis, Davidson 2, Crawley 2	3,200
	5	(a)	Birmingham	D	0-0		1,000
	8	(h)	W.B.A.	W	4-0	Murray 3, Davidson	3,998

LEAGUE CUP

Apr	20	(h)	Luton Town	W	3-0	Davidson, Taylor 2	5,089
	27	(a)	Luton Town	L	1-2	Davidson	4,000
May	4	(a)	Wolves	W	2-0	Lowrie 2	6,035
	11	(h)	Wolves	W	5-2	Crawley, Lowrie 2, Davidson 2	8,713
	18	(h)	W.B.A.	L	0-1	(aet)	7,821

Appearances (League & Cup): L. Armeson 3, G.H. Ashall 5, J. Astley 29, H. Barratt 3, H.A. Boileau 31, L. Coen 3, T. Crawley 34, R.T. Davidson 17, C.S. Elliott 13, W. Frith 30, T. Green 25, E.W. Lager 3, J. Lauderdale 4*, I.S. Lewis 10, G. Lowrie 21, G.W. Mason 30, W.F. Metcalf 25, W. Morgan 24, D. Murray 4*, B. Smith 6, N. Smith 1, J. Snape 12, G.T. Taylor 24, L.H. Warner 23, A.R. Wood 12 — **Total 396.** * *Guest player.*

Goalscorers (L & C): Crawley 24, Davidson 15, Green 11, Lowrie 10, Taylor 7, Frith 5, Murray 5, Barratt 5, Lager 2, Lauderdale 2, Lewis 1, Mason 1 — **Total 87.**

RECORD

P	W	D	L	F	A
36	17	5	14	87	68

Season 1940-41

FOOTBALL LEAGUE (SOUTH)

Aug	31	(h)	Leicester C	D	1-1	Lowrie	1,545
Sep	7	(a)	Leicester C	W	2-0	Crawley, Lowrie	2,106
	14	(h)	Reading	W	7-3	Crawley 2, Lowrie 3, Lauderdale 2	2,517
	21	(a)	Reading	L	2-3	Frith, Crawley	2,066
	28	(h)	Notts County	D	1-1	Elliott	1,967
Oct	5	(a)	Notts County	W	3-1	Taylor, Crawley 2	2,114
	12	(h)	Cardiff City	W	5-2	Ashall, Davidson, Taylor, Mason, Crawley	2,535
	19	(a)	Cardiff City	D	2-2	O'Brien, Frith	5,090
Nov	2	(h)	Northampton T	L	1-2	Lowrie	307
	9	(a)	W.B.A.	W	4-1	Lowrie, O'Brien, Ashall, Crawley	978

* No more games played after mid-November owing to Coventry's ground at Highfield Road being bombed by enemy aircraft.

Appearances (League & Cup): L.R. Armeson 2, G.H. Ashall 4, H.A. Boileau 9, T. Crawley 10, R.T. Davidson 8, C.S. Elliott 9, W. Frith 7, L.J. Jones 1, J.H. Lauderdale 4, I.S. Lewis 1, G. Lowrie 7, G.W. Mason 10, W.F. Metcalf 10, W. Morgan 7, D. Murray 1*, R.V. O'Brien 7, G.T. Taylor 10, A.R. Wood 3 — **Total 110.** * *Guest player.*

Goalscorers (L & C): Crawley 8, Lowrie 7, Ashall 2, Frith 2, Lauderdale 2, O'Brien 2, Taylor 2, Davidson 1, Elliott 1, Mason 1 — **Total 28.**

RECORD

P	W	D	L	F	A
10	5	3	2	28	16

Coventry City did not play competitive football in season 1941-42.

Tommy Green, formerly of West Bromwich Albion and West Ham, scored 11 goals for Coventry in 1939-40, four against his old club, the Baggies.

Coventry City

Season 1942-43

FOOTBALL LEAGUE NORTH

Aug	29	(a)	Walsall	L	0-1		2,000
Sep	5	(h)	Walsall	W	1-0	Crawley	6,356
	12	(h)	Aston Villa	W	2-1	Crawley 2	14,720
	19	(a)	Aston Villa	D	1-1	Crawley	16,000
	26	(a)	Leicester C	D	0-0		6,025
Oct	3	(h)	Leicester C	W	5-1	Ashall, Lowrie 3, Simpson	9,575
	10	(h)	Northampton T	W	5-0	Lowrie 4, Bolan	10,814
	17	(a)	Northampton T	W	2-1	Young, Murray	3,076
	24	(h)	Birmingham	D	2-2	Crawley, Mason	8,638
	31	(a)	Birmingham	L	0-1		5,000
Nov	7	(h)	Wolves	W	1-0	Lowrie	10,257
	14	(a)	Wolves	D	1-1	Armeson	4,904
	21	(a)	Northampton T	W	2-1	Crawley, Simmons	4,114
	28	(h)	Northampton T	W	2-1	Lee, Lowrie	6,936
Dec	5	(a)	Walsall	D	1-1	O'Brien	2,500
	12	(h)	Walsall	W	1-0	Crawley	6,111
	19	(h)	W.B.A.	W	2-1	Crawley 2	5,043
	25	(a)	W.B.A.	L	0-3		5,199
Mar	20	(a)	Birmingham	W	2-1	Simmons, Lowrie	1,000
	27	(h)	Birmingham	W	2-1	Barratt, Lowrie	4,864
Apr	3	(a)	Derby County	D	1-1	Lager	6,000
	10	(h)	Derby County	L	0-1		6,034
	17	(a)	Leicester C	W	3-1	Lowrie 2, Simmons	3,556
	24	(h)	Notts County	W	7-0	Crawley 2, Lowrie 4, Simmons	6,166
	26	(h)	Leicester C	D	0-0		4,556
May	1	(a)	Notts County	L	1-2	Simpson	1,127

LEAGUE CUP

Dec	26	(h)	Walsall	W	2-0	Simmons, Simpson	10,359
Jan	2	(a)	Walsall	W	3-1	Lowrie 2, Crawley	1,997
	9	(a)	W.B.A.	W	3-2	Coen 2, Lowrie	3,676
	16	(h)	W.B.A.	W	1-0	Simmons	8,315
	23	(a)	Northampton T	W	2-0	Lowrie, Simmons	4,024
	30	(h)	Northampton T	L	0-1		8,505
Feb	6	(a)	Leicester C	W	2-0	Setchell, Lowrie	8,187
	13	(h)	Leicester C	L	1-3	Lowrie	9,544
	30	(h)	Birmingham	W	1-0	Lowrie	7,578
	27	(a)	Birmingham	L	1-3	Lager	2,000
Mar	6	(h)	W.B.A.	D	1-1	Crawley	11,502
	13	(a)	W.B.A.	L	0-3		13,332

Appearances (League & Cup): L. Abrahams 1, L.R. Armeson 8, G.H. Ashall 2, G. Bainbridge 1, H. Barratt 17, E. Batchelor 1, S.L. Bennett 2, H.A. Boileau 22, L.A. Bolan 9*, W.A. Bond 3, S.A. Chapman 4, L. Coen 8, C. Craven 1*, T. Crawley 29, C.S. Elliott 29, J.T. Evans 1, W. Frith 21, R. Gardner 1, N.R. Greenway 6, K.H. Grubb 2, R.K. Hartopp 1, C.W.H. Humphries 2, S.R. Kelley 4, E.W. Lager 4, D. Lapworth 1*, J.H. Lauderdale 1*, J. Lee 2, I.S. Lewis 7, G. Lowrie 33, G.W. Mason 35, G.H. Merrick 1*, W.F. Metcalf 13, F. Mitchell 1, W. Morgan 5, D. Murray 4*, R.V. O'Brien 31*, W. Quinton 1*, E. Roberts 1, R. Ryan 2, A.S. Setchell 12, R. Shaw 1*, C.K. Simmons 17, D. Simpson 21, S.W. Smith 6, J. Snape 10, G.T. Taylor 1, J.L. Walker 1, T. Whitecroft 1, A.R. Wood 30, C. Young 1 — **Total 418.**
** Guest player.*

Goalscorers (L & C): Lowrie 24, Crawley 13, Simmons 7, Simpson 3, Coen 2, Lager 2, Armeson 1, Ashall 1, Barratt 1, Bolan 1, Lee 1, Mason 1, Murray 1, O'Brien 1, Setchell 1, Young 1 — **Total 61.**

RECORD

P	W	D	L	F	A
38	21	8	9	61	37

Frank Mitchell (Blues) guested for Coventry City in 1942-43.

George Taylor, ex-Bolton, made 35 'wartime' appearances for Coventry.

Coventry City

Season 1943-44

FOOTBALL LEAGUE (NORTH) FIRST COMPETITION

Aug	28	(a)	Birmingham	D	0-0		7,000
Sep	4	(h)	Birmingham	W	2-1	Crawley, Lowrie	7,929
	11	(h)	Walsall	D	3-3	Lowrie 2, Simpson	6,341
	18	(a)	Walsall	D	1-1	Crawley	2,750
	25	(h)	Leicester C	L	0-1		5,962
Oct	2	(a)	Leicester C	L	0-1		9,108
	9	(a)	Aston Villa	D	0-0		15,000
	16	(h)	Aston Villa	L	0-1		14,014
	23	(a)	Northampton T	W	3-0	Vinall 2, Simpson	12,000
	30	(h)	Northampton T	W	4-1	Gardner 2, Crawley 2	9,200
Nov	6	(a)	Wolves	L	1-2	Barratt	4,006
	13	(h)	Wolves	D	1-1	Lowrie	7,168
	20	(h)	Northampton T	L	0-1		5,320
	27	(a)	Northampton T	L	1-4	Gardner	4,224
Dec	4	(h)	Walsall	L	1-3	Barratt	3,606
	11	(a)	Walsall	D	0-0		2,957
	18	(a)	W.B.A.	L	0-3		2,647
	25	(h)	W.B.A.	W	8-0	Crawley 5, McKeown 2, Barratt	7,398
Apr	1	(a)	Nottingham F	L	1-4	Simpson	5,073
	8	(h)	Nottingham F	W	3-0	Boileau, McKeown, Newbold (aet)	6,432
	10	(h)	Birmingham	L	0-3		5,860
	15	(a)	Leicester C	D	1-1	Edwards	4,037
	22	(h)	Leicester C	W	6-2	Barratt, Crawley 3, Edwards, McKeown	2,099
	29	(a)	Notts County	W	4-1	Setchell, Crawley 2, Barratt	1,540
May	6	(h)	Notts County	W	8-2	Coen, Barratt 4, McKeown 2, Crawley	1,775

FOOTBALL LEAGUE NORTH (2nd COMPETITION)

Dec	26	(h)	Walsall	W	3-0	Mason 2, McKeown	3,700
Jan	1	(a)	Walsall	L	0-3		4,000
	8	(h)	Wolves	W	3-2	Lowrie 3	6,356
	15	(a)	Wolves	D	2-2	Lowrie, Crawley	7,856
	22	(a)	W.B.A.	D	2-2	Crawley 2	5,577
	29	(h)	W.B.A.	D	3-3	Lowrie, McKeown, Crawley	8,500
Feb	5	(a)	Aston Villa	L	0-4		12,000
	12	(h)	Aston Villa	W	2-0	Crawley, Barratt	15,770
	19	(h)	Northampton T	W	2-0	Dennison og, Lowrie	5,701
	26	(a)	Northampton T	W	2-1	Edwards 2	2,102
Mar	4	(a)	Derby County	L	1-2	Lowrie	9,000
	11	(h)	Derby County	W	3-0	Lowrie, McKeown, Coen	12,172
	18	(h)	Aston Villa	L	1-2	Lowrie	23,664
	25	(a)	Aston Villa	L	1-2	Pritchard	25,000

Appearances (League & Cup): L.R. Armeson 2, J. Astley 1, H. Barratt 35, H.A. Boileau 22, W.A. Bond 2, S.A. Chapman 2, L. Coen 22, S.H. Cornwell 9, T. Crawley 34, A. Cryer 1, T. Dougall 2, P. Doyle 1, G. Edwards 25*, C.S. Elliott 33, W. Frith 1, F. Gardner 10*, R. Garner 9, K.L. Green 1, K.H. Grubb 1, H. Hale 1, A. Harris 1*, F. Keeble 1, I.S. Lewis 5, G. Lowrie 19, G.W. Mason 35, J. McKeown 23, W.F. Metcalf 30, J.P. Miles 1, W. Morgan 22, P. Murphy 5, W.G. Nash 2, R. Newbold 1, R.V. O'Brien 25*, H.J. Pritchard 2*, H. Quinney 1, A.G. Setchell 3, C.K. Simmons 4, D. Simpson 10, N. Smith 1, S.W. Smith 3, J. Snape 2, E.J. Vinall 3*, R. Ward 1, L.H. Warner 4, K.C. Watkins 1, A.R. Wood 7, W.C. Wright 3 — **Total 429.** *Guest player.*

Goalscorers (L & C): Crawley 20, Lowrie 13, Barratt 10, McKeown 9, Edwards 4, Gardner 3, Simpson 3, Coen 2, Mason 2, Vinall 2, Boileau 1, Newbold 1, Pritchard 1, Setchell 1, opponent 1 — **Total 73.**

RECORD

P	W	D	L	F	A
39	14	10	15	73	59

Season 1944-45

FOOTBALL LEAGUE (NORTH) FIRST COMPETITION

Aug	26	(a)	Walsall	W	3-2	Lowrie, Currie 2	4,000
Sep	2	(h)	Walsall	W	2-1	Barratt, O'Brien	2,900
	9	(a)	Birmingham	W	2-1	Barratt, Currie	10,000
	16	(h)	Birmingham	L	0-1		9,927
	23	(h)	W.B.A.	D	1-1	Edwards	8,245
	30	(a)	W.B.A.	L	1-4	Lewis	9,512
Oct	7	(a)	Port Vale	L	0-2		6,036
	14	(h)	Port Vale	W	4-3	Paul 3, Elliott	4,957
	21	(a)	Northampton T	L	1-4	Paul	3,125
	28	(h)	Northampton T	W	3-1	Paul, McKeown, Crawley	4,816
Nov	4	(a)	Leicester C	L	1-2	Paul	5,989
	11	(h)	Leicester C	W	3-1	Paul 2, Frith	4,829
	18	(a)	Aston Villa	L	0-4		10,000
	25	(h)	Aston Villa	L	0-6		10,450
Dec	2	(h)	Stoke City	L	0-1		6,405
	9	(a)	Stoke City	L	0-5		4,020
	16	(a)	Wolves	D	1-1	Crawley	6,148
	23	(h)	Wolves	L	1-2	Dougall	5,044
	26	(a)	Birmingham	D	0-0		4,000
Mar	24	(h)	Notts County	W	1-0	Morby og	4,339
	31	(a)	Notts County	W	2-1	Faulkner, Elliott	2,007
Apr	7	(a)	Nottingham F	D	1-1	Crawley	4,000
	14	(h)	Nottingham F	D	1-1	Jarvis	3,188
	21	(a)	Birmingham	W	2-1	Elliott 2	8,015
	28	(h)	Birmingham	D	2-2	Elliott, Faulkner	3,867
May	5	(a)	Aston Villa	L	2-9	Faulkner, Dougall	8,000
	12	(h)	Aston Villa	W	3-1	Lewis, Jones, Dougall	5,130

FOOTBALL LEAGUE NORTH SECOND COMPETITION

Dec	30	(a)	W.B.A.	D	1-1	Dougall	8,659
Jan	6	(a)	Birmingham	L	1-5	Merrick og	12,000
	13	(h)	Birmingham	L	1-2	Crawley	5,084
	20	(a)	Walsall	L	5-6	Crawley 3, Dougall 2	1,095
	27	(h)	Walsall	L	0-2		2,667
Feb	3	(h)	Aston Villa	L	2-3	McKeown, Elliott	7,017
	10	(a)	Aston Villa	L	2-4	Dougall, Smith	12,000
	17	(a)	Northampton T	L	1-8	Edwards	7,128
	24	(h)	Northampton T	W	3-0	Crawley, Edwards, Dougall	4,959
Mar	3	(h)	W.B.A.	L	0-3		7,048
	10	(h)	Notts County	W	4-0	Edwards, Elliott 2, Currie	3,166
	17	(a)	Leicester C	D	2-2	Elliott, Edwards	5,133

Appearances (League & Cup): L.R. Armeson 5, H. Barratt 10, H.A. Boileau 8, J.C. Bowles 14*, T. Brown 1, W.J. Carey 8*, J. Cook 4, F. Copson 2, T. Crawley 36, A. Currie 6, C. Dougall 18*, T. Dougall 1, F.L. Douglas 1, G. Edwards 33, C.S. Elliott 31, J. Evans 3, K. Faulkner 13*, J. Fitzpatrick 1, W. Frith 17, R. Garner 15, T. Green 15, J.H. Jarvis 1*, L.J. Jones 7*, S.R. Kelley 2, J.T. Kendall 11, D. Kerry 7, J. King 2*, G. Lewis 2*, I.S. Lewis 9, G. Lowrie 1, G.W. Mason 33, A. McKeown 1, J. McKeown 15, W.F. Metcalf 19, A. Morton 1, R.V. O'Brien 28*, R.G. Paul 10, F.H. Robinson 1, R.A. Ryan 4, A.G. Setchell 1, C.K. Simmons 3, D. Simpson 4, C. Smith 1*, J. Snape 4, F.W. Taylor 4, R.A. Ward 11, L.H. Warner 1, K. Watkins 4 — **Total 429.** *Guest player.*

Goalscorers (L & C): Elliott 9, Crawley 8, Dougall 8, Paul 8, Edwards 5, Currie 4, Faulkner 3, Barratt 2, Lewis 2, McKeown 2, opponents 2, Frith 1, Jarvis 1, Jones 1, Lowrie 1, O'Brien 1, Smith 1 — **Total 59.**

RECORD

P	W	D	L	F	A
39	12	8	19	59	94

Coventry City

Season 1945-46

FOOTBALL LEAGUE (SOUTH)

Aug	25	(h)	Arsenal	W	2-0	Gardner, Lowrie	20,943
Sep	1	(a)	Arsenal	D	0-0		28,000
	8	(a)	Charlton Ath	L	1-3	Lowrie	15,600
	15	(h)	Charlton Ath	D	1-1	Barratt	15,520
	17	(h)	Birmingham	L	2-3	Barratt 2	14,416
	22	(h)	Fulham	W	3-1	Matthews, Lowrie, Barratt	12,047
	29	(a)	Fulham	L	0-2		21,898
Oct	6	(h)	Plymouth A	W	3-1	Small 2, Lowrie	12,750
	13	(a)	Plymouth A	D	1-1	Lowrie	18,128
	20	(h)	Portsmouth	W	3-1	Barratt, Aldecoa, Small	13,621
	27	(a)	Portsmouth	D	1-1	Lowrie	18,554
Nov	3	(a)	Nottingham F	D	0-0		10,107
	10	(h)	Nottingham F	L	1-4	Pritchard	10,920
	15	(h)	Newport Co.	W	7-1	Barrett 3, Lowrie, Simpson 2, Small	9,133
Dec	1	(a)	Wolves	L	0-1		19,730
	8	(h)	Wolves	W	1-0	Simpson	13,824
	15	(h)	West Ham	L	2-5	Barratt, Crawley	11,719
	22	(a)	West Ham	L	3-6	Lowrie, Simpson, Fenton og	14,128
	24	(a)	W.B.A.	D	2-2	Roberts, O'Brien	18,038
	26	(h)	W.B.A.	W	3-2	Aldecoa 2, Barratt	19,303
	29	(a)	Birmingham	L	0-2		24,107
Jan	12	(h)	Brentford	W	1-0	Warner	13,450
	19	(a)	Brentford	W	2-1	Owens 2	10,309
	26	(a)	Tottenham	L	0-2		17,995
Feb	2	(h)	Chelsea	L	2-0	Aldecoa, Barratt	19,289
	9	(h)	Millwall	W	7-2	Barratt 4, Bilbao, Aldecoa, Simpson	10,004
	16	(a)	Millwall	D	1-1	Barratt	17,535
	23	(a)	Southampton	L	3-4	Barratt 3	10,113
Mar	2	(h)	Southampton	L	0-1		11,811
	14	(h)	Derby County	W	3-1	Roberts 2, Barratt	14,246
	16	(a)	Derby County	L	0-3		19,974
	23	(a)	Leicester C	W	3-1	Barratt 2, Crawley	13,864
	30	(h)	Leicester C	L	0-1		14,240
Apr	6	(h)	Swansea	D	2-2	Barratt, Metcalf	12,993
	10	(a)	Chelsea	L	1-2	Barratt	10,000
	13	(a)	Swansea Town	L	2-3	Crawley 2	23,056
	19	(a)	Luton Town	W	2-1	Roberts, Barratt	16,340
	20	(a)	Aston Villa	D	0-0		40,000
	22	(h)	Luton Town	L	0-3		14,282
	27	(h)	Aston Villa	D	2-2	Aldecoa, Lowrie	12,968
May	4	(h)	Tottenham	L	0-1		11,446
		(a)	Newport Co.	W	3-1	Barratt, Lowrie 2	6,000

F.A. CUP

Jan	5	(h)	Aston Villa	R3/1	2-1	Barratt, Simpson	27,197
	8	(a)	Aston Villa	R3/2	0-2		20,000

Appearances (League): E. Aldecoa 30, G.H. Ashall 1, H. Barratt 42, J. Bilbao 5, A. Calverley 1*, T. Crawley 41, R.T. Davidson 4, T. Dougall 1, T. Eggleston 1*, C.S. Elliott 31, F.C. Gardner 16*, R. Goddard 1*, A. Harris 1*, W.E. Houghton 1*, D. Johnson 2*, L.J. Jones 2*, S.R. Kelley 15, D. Kelly 4, J. Kendall 1, I.S. Lewis 2, J. Loughran 1*, G. Lowrie 21, C.C. Lyman 1*, G.W. Mason 33, H. Matthews 5, A. McKeown 2, J. McKeown 1, W.F. Metcalf 34, R.V. O'Brien 9*, T.L. Owens 2*, H.J. Pritchard 7, E. Roberts 15, A.G. Setchell 3, D. Simpson 23, S.J. Small 8*, C. Smith 2*, J. Snape 19, R. Ward 2, L.H. Warner 22, K.C. Watkins 8, A.R. Wood 42 — **Total 462.** * *Guest player.*

Goalscorers (L): Barratt 26, Lowrie 11, Aldecoa 6, Simpson 5, Crawley 4, Roberts 4, Small 4, Owens 2, Bilbao 1, Gardner 1, Matthews 1, Metcalf 1, O'Brien 1, Pritchard 1, Warner 1, opponent 1 — **Total 70.**

F.A. Cup appearances: E. Aldecoa 2, H. Barratt 2, T. Crawley 2, C.S. Elliott 2, G. Mason 2, H. Matthews 2, W. Metcalf 2, D. Simpson 2, J. Snape 1, R. Ward 1, L. Warner 2, A. Wood 2 — **Total 22.**

F.A. Cup goalscorers: Barratt 1, Simpson 1 — **Total 2.**

RECORD

	P	W	D	L	F	A	Pts
League(s)	42	15	10	17	70	69	40
F.A.C.	2	1	0	1	2	1	—
Total	44	16	10	18	72	70	

TOP WARTIME APPEARANCES

T. Crawley	186
G.W. Mason	178
C.S. Elliott	148
W.F. Metcalf	133
H. Barratt	109
R.V. O'Brien	100
G. Lowrie	103
A. Wood	96
A.H. Boileau	92
W. Frith	76
D. Simpson	60
G. Edwards	58
W. Morgan	58
T. Green	40
G. Taylor	35
E. Aldecoa	32

TOP WARTIME GOALSCORERS

T. Crawley	77
G. Lowrie	66
H. Barratt	45
R.T. Davidson	16
D. Simpson	12
T. Green	11
McKeown	11
C.S. Elliott	10
G. Edwards	9
G. Taylor	9
Dougall	8
Frith	8
Paul	8
C.K. Simmons	7

Coventry's complete Wartime Record

Season	**P**	**W**	**D**	**L**	**F**	**A**
1939-40	36	17	5	14	87	68
1940-41	10	5	3	2	28	16
1941-42	Did not compete					
1942-43	38	21	8	9	61	37
1943-44	39	14	10	15	73	59
1944-45	39	12	8	19	59	94
1945-46(L)	42	15	10	17	70	67
1945-46(C)	2	1	—	1	2	3
Total	206	85	44	77	380	344

George Mason, hard-man of the Coventry defence, made 178 appearances for City during the war.

Walsall

Season 1939-40

FOOTBALL LEAGUE DIVISION 3 (SOUTH)

Aug	26	(a)	Southend	L	2-3	Alsop, Bulger	6,000
	30	(a)	Torquay Utd	D	0-0		5,000
Sep	2	(h)	Q.P.R.	W	1-0	Bulger	5,000

REGIONAL LEAGUE (MIDLAND DIVISION)

Oct	21	(a)	Leicester City	L	1-6	Alsop	1,600
	28	(h)	Birmingham	L	1-2	Taylor	4,554
Nov	4	(a)	Wolves	L	1-4	Brown	4,517
	11	(h)	Northampton T	D	1-1	Bulger	2,730
	18	(h)	Luton Town	L	4-6	Brown 3, Alsop	2,347
	25	(a)	Coventry C	L	3-4	Taylor, Alsop 2	2,000
Dec	2	(h)	W.B.A.	L	0-2		4,815
	9	(h)	Leicester C	W	4-3	Alsop 2, Wood, Bulger	1,645
	16	(a)	Birmingham	L	1-2	Brown	2,464
	23	(h)	Wolves	L	3-5	Brown, Wood, Alsop	5,448
	30	(a)	Northampton T	L	1-6	Alsop	6,929
Jan	1	(a)	Luton Town	L	0-1		529
	13	(h)	Coventry C	L	0-2		1,720
	20	(a)	W.B.A.	L	2-7	Male, Brown	1,831
Feb	24	(h)	Luton Town	D	4-4	Starling, Alsop 3	1,794
Mar	2	(a)	Coventry C	L	1-4	Alsop	1,528
	9	(h)	W.B.A.	D	1-1	White (og)	3,012
	16	(h)	Leicester C	W	3-2	Alsop 2, Edwards	2,509
	23	(a)	Birmingham	L	1-2	Alsop	13,241
	30	(h)	Wolves	L	1-2	Brown	6,106
Apr	6	(a)	Northampton T	D	2-2	Hancocks, Brown	3,022
May	4	(a)	Luton Town	W	4-3	Brown, Alsop, Bulger, Hancocks	1,212
	11	(h)	Northampton T	W	1-0	Alsop	2,000
	14	(a)	W.B.A.	W	3-2	Wood 2, Alsop	1,567
	18	(a)	Wolves	W	5-1	Bulger, Alsop 3, Wood	5,038
	25	(h)	Coventry City	W	2-1	Alsop, Wood	2,700
June	1	(a)	Leicester C	D	0-0		4,000
	8	(a)	Birmingham	L	1-8	Alsop	1,000

LEAGUE CUP

Apr	13	(a)	Port Vale	D	2-2	Alsop 2	2,000
	15	(h)	Port Vale	W	6-0	Dryden 2, Alsop 2, Hancocks, Hickman	1,500
	20	(a)	Swansea Town	L	0-2		5,040
	27	(h)	Swansea Town	W	2-1	Brown, Wood	3,821

Appearances (League & Cup): R. Adams 1, G. Alsop 35, J.M. Beattie 7*, J.H. Beesley 1, G. Beeson 2, T.F. Biddlestone 9*, W.S. Brown 29*, C.G. Bulger 29, A. Buttery 1*, I Clarke 1*, J. Dryden 5*, G.R. Edwards 4*, F.T. Fisher 1*, C. Godfrey 34, A.T. Grosvenor 2, J. Hancocks 25, K. Harper 2, J.A. Hickman 7*, N.A. Male 32, L.D. Morgan 26, D. Richards 23, J.B.T. Shelton 19, R.W. Starling 3*, G.J. Strong 3, F.L. Talbot 3, T. Taylor 9, W. Thayne 20, G. Walton 3, B.F. Williams 23, T. Wood 26* — **Total 385.** * *Guest player.*

Goalscorers (L & C): Alsop 28, Brown 10, Wood 7, Bulger 6, Hancocks 4, Dryden 2, Taylor 2, Edwards 1, Hickman 1, Male 1, Starling 1, opponent 1 — **Total 64.**

RECORD

P	W	D	L	F	A
35	10	7	18	64	91

Season 1940-41

REGIONAL LEAGUE (SOUTH)

Aug	31	(a)	W.B.A.	L	1-3	Vinall	2,966
Sep	7	(h)	W.B.A.	L	0-2		2,968
	14	(a)	Bristol City	L	0-2		2,000
	21	(h)	Bristol City	W	4-1	Walton, Beesley, Vinall 2	1,546
	28	(a)	Nottingham F	L	0-2		1,500
Oct	5	(h)	Nottingham F	W	4-3	Beesley, Starling, Walton, Vinall	2,014
	12	(h)	Notts County	W	3-2	Starling, Vinall 2	3,000
	19	(a)	Notts County	L	2-4	Vinall, Beesley	1,500
	26	(a)	Mansfield T	D	6-6	Vinall 2, Beesley, Hancocks 2, Richards	1,500
Nov	2	(h)	Mansfield T	L	1-3	Brown	520
	9	(h)	Notts County	W	11-4	Rowley 4, Brown 2, Vinall 4, Wood	427
	16	(a)	Notts County	L	1-2	Brown	1,053
	23	(h)	Leicester C	W	5-0	Hancocks 2, Brown, Rowley 2	1,472
	30	(a)	Leicester C	D	1-1	Brown	600
Dec	21	(a)	Stoke City	D	2-2	Starling, Rowley	540
	25	(h)	Birmingham	W	6-3	Vinall 2, Rowley 4	2,891
	28	(h)	Stoke City	W	5-1	Vinall 3, Rowley 2	3,518
Mar	29	(a)	W.B.A.	L	1-4	Wood	1,412
Apr	5	(h)	W.B.A.	D	3-3	Hancocks 2, Vinall	1,850
	19	(h)	Mansfield T	D	1-1	Hancocks	1,495
	26	(a)	Mansfield T	D	2-2	Harkin, Rickards	522
May	10	(h)	Leicester C	W	3-1	Brown, Thayne, Hancocks	1,250
	24	(h)	Nottingham F	L	6-7	Rowley 4, Vinall, Hancocks	1,038
	31	(h)	W.B.A.	W	10-3	Beesley 2, Vinall, Rowley 4, Hancocks 2, Starling	1,512

MIDLAND CUP

Jan	4	(a)	Luton Town	L	2-6	Vinall, Rowley	517
	11	(h)	Luton Town	W	3-2	Vinall 2, Rowley	2,500
Feb	8	(h)	W.B.A.	W	4-3	Hancocks, Vinall, Brown 2	3,135
	15	(h)	Nottingham F	W	3-2	Brown, Alsop, Brook (og)	2,910
	22	(a)	Nottingham F	L	1-8	Starling	1,520
Mar	1	(a)	Stoke City	D	1-1	Brown	1,045
	8	(h)	Stoke City	W	7-3	Brown 2, Starling 2, Dryden 2, Vinall	1,616
	15	(a)	Northampton T	W	3-1	Wrigglesworth, Starling, Vinall	2,500
	22	(h)	Northampton T	W	2-0	Hancocks, Dryden	2,566
May	3	(a)	Leicester C	L	0-2	(FINAL)	7,000

Appearances (League & Cup): G. Alsop 2, J.H. Beesley 13, T.F. Biddlestone 32*, W.S. Brown 27, C.G. Bulger 1, J. Dryden 7*, C. Godfrey 32, J. Hancocks 27, G.T. Jones 1, N.A. Male 31, L.D. Morgan 27, D. Richards 19, J.F. Rowley 14*, J.B.T. Shelton 32, R.W. Starling 33*, W. Thayne 8, E.J. Vinall 30*, G. Walton 5, B.F. Williams 1, T. Wood 31*, W. Wrigglesworth 1* — **Totals: 374.** * *Guest player.*

Goalscorers (L & C): Vinall 27, Rowley 23, Hancocks 13, Brown 13, Starling 8, Beesley 6, Dryden 3, Walton 2, Richards 1, Thayne 1, Wood 2, Wrigglesworth 1, Alsop 1, Harkin 1, Rickards 1, opponent 1 — **Total 104.**

RECORD

P	W	D	L	F	A
34	15	7	12	104	90

Walsall's Cup Final team against Leicester City on 3rd May 1941 was: Biddlestone; Shelton, Male, Wood, Morgan, Godfrey, Hancocks, Vinall, Thayne, Starling, Beesley.

Gilbert Alsop (left) in action for Walsall during the war.

Walsall

Season 1941-42

FOOTBALL LEAGUE (SOUTH)

Aug	30	(a)	Northampton T	L	2-3	Dennison (og), Vinall	2,016
Sep	6	(h)	Northampton T	D	2-2	Starling, Brown,	2,508
	13	(a)	Swansea T	W	7-4	Beesley 2, Wood, Vinall, Shelton, Brown 2	4,000
	20	(h)	Swansea T	W	4-2	Brown 2, Vinall, Beesley	2,500
	27	(h)	W.B.A.	W	2-1	Shell, Starling	4,494
Oct	4	(a)	W.B.A.	L	0-4		4,135
	11	(h)	Nottingham F	W	8-2	Starling, Wood 2, Batty 2, Hancocks 2, Vinall	2,500
	18	(a)	Nottingham F	L	0-4		1,063
	25	(a)	Wolves	L	0-1		3,527
Nov	1	(h)	Wolves	W	4-1	Brown 2, Ashley, Shell	2,408
	8	(h)	Leicester C	W	2-1	Wood, Hancocks	3,000
	15	(a)	Leicester C	L	0-6		4,000
	22	(h)	Bristol City	W	5-0	Vinall 3, Beesley, Batty	2,000
	29	(a)	Bristol City	L	2-4	Vinall, Wood	2,500
Dec	6	(a)	Luton Town	W	2-1	Ashley, Wilkie	1,000
	13	(h)	Luton Town	W	5-3	Beesley 2, Ashley, Vinall 2	1,500
	20	(h)	Wolves	L	1-2	Vinall	1,529
	25	(a)	Wolves	L	3-4	Vinall 2, Beesley	3,895
Apr	11	(h)	Stoke City	W	1-0	Vinall	1,047
	18	(a)	Stoke city	W	3-2	Dudley, Newsome, Ashley	1,500
May	23	(a)	W.B.A.	L	1-3	Newsome	1,695

LEAGUE CUP QUALIFYING GAMES

Dec	27	(h)	Stoke City	L	1-4	Vinall	3,000
Jan	3	(a)	Stoke City	L	0-8		3,000
	10	(a)	Northampton T	L	1-6	Vinall	3,000
	17	(h)	Northampton T	L	1-3	Beesley	1,500
	31	(a)	Chester	L	3-4	Alsop, Embleton, Beesley	1,000
Feb	14	(h)	Chester	L	0-2		1,059
	21	(a)	Wrexham	L	0-1		996
	28	(h)	Wrexham	W	2-0	Vinall 2	1,055
Mar	21	(h)	Mansfield T	W	1-0	Newsome	874
	28	(a)	Mansfield T	L	0-2		627

Appearances (League & Cup): G. Alsop 2, J. Arnold 1, H. Ashley 14*, D.W. Auckland 2*, G. Ball 4, S.G. Batty 10*, J.H. Beesley 26, T.F. Biddlestone 29*, W.S. Brown 11, C.G. Bulger 9, V. Coles 1*, G. Dudley 5*, C. Duffy 3*, S.E. Dyall 4, E. Embleton 2*, C.J. Evans 1*, C. Godfrey 19, J. Hancocks 7, R. Holland 4, L. Jarvis 9, H. Lane 1*, J. Lewis 4*, I. Lord 1*, N.A. Male 17, L.D. Morgan 27, R. Newsome 5*, W.G. Richardson 1*, F. Roberts 1*, F.H. Shell 6*, J.B.T. Shelton 31, A.J. Smith 1*, R.W. Starling 20*, W. Thayne 5, A.R. Tranter 3*, E.J. Vinall 24*, C.H. Wilkie 2*, B.F. Williams 2, T. Wood 27* — **Total 341.** ** Guest player.*

Goalscorers (L & C): Vinall 18, Beesley 9, Brown 7, Wood 5, Ashley 4, Batty 3, Hancocks 3, Newsome 3, Starling 3, Shell 2, Alsop 1, Dudley 1, Embleton 1, Shelton 1, Wilkie 1 — **Total 63.**

RECORD

P	W	D	L	F	A
31	13	1	17	63	79

George Dudley

(ex W.B.A.)

Season 1942-43

FOOTBALL LEAGUE NORTH (1st COMPETITION)

Aug	29	(h)	Coventry C	W	1-0	Wood	2,000
Sep	5	(a)	Coventry C	L	0-1		6,356
	12	(a)	Northampton T	L	2-4	Alsop, Brown	2,337
	19	(h)	Northampton T	L	0-2		2,042
	26	(a)	Aston Villa	D	2-2	Vinall, Wood	7,500
Oct	3	(h)	Aston Villa	W	3-0	Brown, Newsome 2	4,500
	10	(a)	Wolves	L	2-3	Brown 2	6,105
	17	(h)	Wolves	W	5-2	Vinall 2, Newsome, Dudley, Brown	4,990
	24	(h)	Northampton T	W	6-0	Ashley, Newsome 2, Wood, Brown 2	2,000
	31	(a)	Northampton T	D	2-2	Vinall, Tranter	4,000
Nov	7	(a)	Birmingham	L	3-4	Wood 2, Brown	4,000
	14	(h)	Birmingham	W	1-0	Brown	2,500
	21	(a)	W.B.A.	D	0-0		2,783
	28	(h)	W.B.A.	W	2-0	Lewis, Ireland	3,412
Dec	5	(h)	Coventry C	D	1-1	Vinall	2,500
	12	(a)	Coventry C	L	0-1		6,111
	19	(a)	Stoke City	L	1-7	Nicholls	519
	25	(h)	Stoke City	D	2-2	Tranter 2	2,229
Mar	6	(h)	Birmingham	L	1-2	Arnold	1,500
	13	(a)	Birmingham	L	1-2	Nicholls	700
Mar	20	(a)	Northampton T	W	4-2	Nicholls 2, Dudley, Martin	1,500
	27	(h)	Northampton T	L	2-5	Martin, Nicholls	988
Apr	17	(a)	W.B.A.	L	0-4		1,575
	24	(h)	W.B.A.	L	1-2	Streten	1,500

FOOTBALL LEAGUE NORTH (2nd COMPETITION)

Dec	26	(a)	Coventry C	L	0-2		10,359
Jan	2	(h)	Coventry C	L	1-3	Nicholls	1,997
	9	(a)	Northampton T	D	2-2	Doherty 2	4,000
	16	(h)	Northampton T	W	2-0	Nicholls, Mason	2,500
	23	(h)	Birmingham	D	1-1	Tranter	3,000
	30	(a)	Birmingham	L	0-1		1,000
Feb	6	(a)	Stoke City	L	1-2	Ashley	4,000
	13	(h)	Stoke City	W	4-1	Nicholls 3, Newsome	3,000
	20	(a)	Aston Villa	L	1-2	Nicholls	12,000
	27	(h)	Aston Villa	L	1-4	Ashley	7,000

Appearances (League & Cup): G. Alsop 1, H. Ashley 17*, G. Ball 1, S.G. Batty 17*, J.H. Beesley 5, D.H. Bilton 6*, W.S. Brown 16, A.E. Bullock 1*, I. Clarke 2*, G.E. Collins 1*, D.M. Colquhoun 1*, M.M. Dickie 1, P. Dickie 5*, P.D. Doherty 1*, G. Dudley 14*, M. Dunkley 5*, D.L. Emmanuel 6*, J. Featherstone 3, D. Grainger 1*, J. Hancocks 3, L. Hann 3*, K. Harper 3*, A. Hickman 2*, E. Hird 1*, H.W. Ireland 2*, L. Jarvis 10, J. Lewis 24*, W.M. Lindley 2*, N.A. Male 24, E. Martin 3, D.W. Mason 2*, W.S. Mason 1*, T.G. Mitchell 6, L.D. Morgan 24, R. Newsome 21*, H. Nicholls 14*, I.V. Powell 3*, M. Reid 1, M.W. Reid 1, F.H. Rist 1*, D.W. Russell 1*, J.B.T. Shelton 30, B.R. Streten 1, C. Timms 1, A.R. Tranter 17, P.G. Vause 6*, E.J. Vinall 16*, J. Watts 2*, H. Wilkinson 2*, B.F. Williams 25, T. Wood 17* — **Total 373.** ** Guest player.*

Goalscorers (L & C): Nicholls 11, Brown 9, Newsome 6, Vinall 5, Wood 5, Tranter 4, Ashley 3, Doherty 2, Dudley 2, Martin 2, Alsop 1, Ireland 1, Lewis 1, Mason 1, Tranter 1, Streten 1 — **Total 55.** ** Guest player.*

RECORD

P	W	D	L	F	A
34	9	7	18	55	66

Johnny Hancocks

Norman Male

Walsall

Season 1943-44

FOOTBALL LEAGUE NORTH (1st COMPETITION)

Aug	28	(a)	Northampton T	L	0-2		3,000
Sep	4	(h)	Northampton T	D	0-0		3,000
	11	(a)	Coventry C	D	3-3	Brown 2, Alsop	6,341
	18	(h)	Coventry C	D	1-1		2,750
	25	(h)	Aston Villa	L	0-2		7,000
Oct	2	(a)	Aston Villa	D	4-4	Alsop 2, Wood, Morby (og)	12,000
	9	(a)	Northampton T	L	0-2		4,000
	16	(h)	Northampton T	D	0-0		3,000
	23	(h)	Wolves	L	1-3	Reid	3,794
	30	(a)	Wolves	D	1-1	Alsop	11,829
Nov	6	(h)	Birmingham	L	2-4	Brown, Hinsley	3,500
	13	(a)	Birmingham	L	1-5	Dudley	3,000
	20	(h)	W.B.A.	W	2-0	Hinsley, Rickman	4,297
	27	(a)	W.B.A.	W	4-1	Hinsley 3, Brown	4,556
Dec	4	(a)	Coventry C	W	3-1	Brown 2, Hinsley	3,606
	11	(h)	Coventry C	D	0-0		2,957
	18	(h)	Stoke City	W	4-2	Batty, Roberts, Brown 2	1,147
	25	(a)	Stoke City	W	1-0	Brown	6,022
Mar	11	(h)	Notts County	W	2-1	Hinsley, Lewis	2,500
	18	(h)	Nottingham F	D	0-0		1,984
	25	(a)	Nottingham F	L	0-2		5,638
Apr	1	(h)	W.B.A.	D	2-2	Bulger, Hinsley	2,120
	8	(a)	W.B.A.	L	0-1		5,588
	15	(h)	Birmingham	D	2-2	Harper, McCormick	2,000
	22	(a)	Birmingham	L	0-5		4,000

FOOTBALL LEAGUE NORTH (2nd COMPETITION)

Dec	26	(a)	Coventry C	L	0-3		3,700
Jan	1	(h)	Coventry C	W	3-0	Dudley 3	4,000
	8	(h)	W.B.A.	D	2-2	Hinsley, Dudley	5,793
	15	(a)	W.B.A.	L	1-7	Batty	4,800
	22	(h)	Northampton T	W	3-0	Welsh 2, Hinsley	3,000
	29	(a)	Northampton T	L	0-2		3,000
Feb	5	(a)	Stoke City	L	1-5	Brown	4,000
	12	(h)	Stoke City	L	0-2		1,986
	19	(h)	Wolves	D	0-0		2,188
	26	(a)	Wolves	D	1-1	Hinsley	3,885

Appearances (League & Cup): G. Alsop 10, S.G. Batty 31*, W.S. Brown 27, C.G. Bulger 1, F. Childs 1, T. Cooper 3, C. Dougall 7*, G. Dudley 16*, D.L. Emmanuel 22*, J. Featherstone 2, E.O. Griffiths 3, J. Hancocks 3, R. Hardy 1*, K. Harper 1, L.E. Hayward 1*, G. Hinsley 23*, G.A. Jackson 1, L. Jarvis 3, B. Jones 1*, J. Lewis 33*, H. Lowery 8*, N.A. Male 30, J. Maund 4*, J. McCormick 2*, J. McKenna 1*, L.D. Morgan 2, W. Mullen 6*, E. Mulligan 2, R. Newsome 1*, H. Nicholls 5*, N. Penrose 3*, W.M. Reid 3, F.W. Rickman 7, F.H. Rist 25*, N.E. Roberts 8*, J.B.T. Shelton 35, B.R. Streten 3, J. Taylor 1, A.R. Tranter 1, P.G. Vause 3*, A. Welsh 3, B.F. Williams 35, T. Wood 6*, E.V. Wright 1* — **Total 385.** ** Guest player.*

Goalscorers (L & C): Hinsley 11, Brown 10, Dudley 5, Alsop 4, Batty 2, Welsh 2, Bulger 1, Harper 1, Lewis 1, McCormick 1, Penrose 1, Reid 1, Rickman 1, Roberts 1, Wood 1, opponent 1 — **Total 44.**

RECORD

P	W	D	L	F	A
35	8	13	14	44	66

Season 1944-45

FOOTBALL LEAGUE NORTH (1st CHAMPIONSHIP)

Aug	26	(h)	Coventry C	L	2-3	Boonham 2	4,000
Sep	2	(a)	Coventry C	L	1-2	Rickman	2,900
	9	(a)	Leicester C	W	3-2	Beech, Kendrick, White	7,000
	16	(h)	Leicester C	L	0-1		5,000
	23	(a)	Aston Villa	D	1-1	Hinsley	18,000
	30	(h)	Aston Villa	L	0-2		9,000
Oct	7	(h)	Stoke City	D	1-1	Vinall	5,000
	14	(a)	Stoke City	W	2-0	Vinall, Hobbis	4,000
	21	(a)	Wolves	D	1-1	Vinall	9,697
	28	(h)	Wolves	L	1-2	Armstrong	7,225
Nov	4	(a)	Northampton T	D	1-1	Shelton	3,000
	11	(h)	Northampton T	W	3-2	Hinsley, Armstrong 2	2,000
	18	(h)	Birmingham	W	4-1	Armstrong 2, Mulligan, Peace	4,500
	25	(a)	Birmingham	D	2-2	Armstrong, Mulligan	5,000
Dec	2	(a)	W.B.A.	L	0-3		8,992
	9	(h)	W.B.A.	L	1-2	Hinsley	5,303
	16	(h)	Port Vale	D	2-2	Alsop 2	2,957
	23	(a)	Port Vale	W	2-1	Ratcliffe, Boonham	4,882
Mar	10	(a)	Wrexham	L	0-1		5,250
	24	(a)	Port Vale	L	2-3	Archibald, Alsop	6,000
	31	(h)	Port Vale	W	2-0	Peace, Lewis	1,500
Apr	2	(a)	Mansfield T	L	0-2		4,000
	7	(a)	W.B.A.	D	1-1	Beech	5,227
	14	(h)	W.B.A.	L	1-2	Snape	1,780
May	5	(h)	Mansfield T	W	4-2	Alsop 4	525

FOOTBALL LEAGUE NORTH (2nd CHAMPIONSHIP)

Dec	26	(a)	Wolves	D	1-1	Boonham	7,759
	30	(a)	Birmingham	L	1-3	Boonham	10,000
Jan	6	(a)	Northampton T	L	1-2	Alsop	5,000
	13	(h)	Northampton T	L	0-1		2,000
	20	(h)	Coventry C	W	6-5	Russell 2, Peace 2, Alsop 2	1,095
	27	(a)	Coventry C	W	2-0	Meath, Pearson	2,667
Feb	3	(a)	W.B.A.	W	2-0	Pearson 2	6,334
	10	(h)	W.B.A.	D	0-0		6,376
	17	(a)	Aston Villa	L	1-6	Alsop	10,000
	24	(h)	Aston Villa	L	0-2		9,894
Mar	3	(h)	Birmingham	L	0-2		4,000

Appearances (League & Cup): G. Alsop 21, C. Archibald 3, M. Armstrong 10*, J. Barker 1*, S.G. Batty 4*, G. Beech 11, H. Beck 1*, G. Billingsley 3*, D.H. Bilton 1*, G. Boonham 5, J. Brown 1*, C.G. Bulger 4, J. Clough 1*, R. Crutchley 8, W.L.W. Flack 1*, G. Forrester 2, J.W. Gallon 2*, A. Gregory 1*, W. Haigh 1*, A. Hall 1*, J. Harper 2*, G. Hinsley 14*, H.H.F. Hobbis 3*, R. Houghton 7*, R.J. Jenkins 8, W. Jessop 2*, J. Johnson 1*, F.C. Kelly 1, K. Kendrick 1*, D.H.G. Kernick 2*, W. Layton 1*, J. Lewis 29*, J.J. Little 2*, H. Lowery 18*, T. Lycett 3*, G. Male 1*, N.A. Male 33, M. McKenna 1*, G. Meath 14, L.D. Morgan 5, J. Morris 1*, W. Mullen 2*, E. Mulligan 9*, H.J. Peace 19, T.U. Pearson 2*, W.T. Peck 1, J. Ratcliffe 2, D.J. Redwood 3*, F.W. Rickman 3, F.H. Rist 21*, D.W. Russell 2*, J.B.T. Shelton 31, A. Smith 1*, H. Snape 1, C. Stone 3, B.R. Streten 5*, E.J. Vinall 26*, F.R.H. White 7*, B.F. Williams 26, T. Wood 1* — **Total 396.** ** Guest player.*

Goalscorers (L & C): Alsop 11, Armstrong 6, Boonham 5, Peace 4, Hinsley 3, Pearson 3, Vinall 3, Beech 2, Mulligan 2, Russell 2, Archibald 1, Hobbis 1, Kernick 1, Lewis 1, Meath 1, Ratcliffe 1, Rickman 1, Shelton 1, Snape 1, White 1 — **Total 51.**

RECORD

P	W	D	L	F	A
36	10	9	17	51	62

Pictured left: Bert Williams and Harry Lowery.

Walsall

Season 1945-46

FOOTBALL LEAGUE DIVISION THREE SOUTH (NORTH)

Aug	25	(a)	Northampton T	D	1-1	Alsop	4,000
Sep	1	(a)	Northampton T	D	0-1		6,000
	8	(a)	Q.P.R.	L	0-4		8,000
	12	(h)	Ipswich Town	W	3-0	Barratt, Alsop, Jenkins	5,000
	15	(h)	Q.P.R.	D	1-1	Hancocks	7,000
	19	(a)	Mansfield T	L	1-6	Vinall	4,000
	22	(h)	Clapton O.	W	5-3	Darby 3, Alsop Hancocks	5,000
	28	(h)	Mansfield T	W	2-0	Bennett 2	3,000
	29	(a)	Clapton O.	L	0-2		4,089
Oct	6	(a)	Watford	L	1-2	Bennett	4,700
	13	(h)	Watford	L	0-3		4,000
Nov	3	(a)	Norwich City	L	1-2	Alsop	7,000
	10	(h)	Norwich City	L	1-2	Bulger	4,000
Dec	1	(a)	Southend Utd	W	1-0	Goffin	6,000
	8	(h)	Southend Utd	W	6-0	Alsop 2, Kelly 4	3,000
	22	(h)	Notts County	D	3-3	Mullard, Hancocks, Kelly	2,553
	24	(a)	Notts County	L	0-2		7,000
	25	(h)	Port Vale	L	1-5	Kelly	2,176
	26	(a)	Port Vale	W	1-0	Foulkes	5,500
	29	(a)	Ipswich Town	L	3-5	Evans, Kelly 2	10,000

F.A. CUP

Nov	17	(a)	Shrewsbury R1/1	0-5		6,531
	24	(h)	Shrewsbury R1/2	4-1	Mullard, Bennett, Talbot, Alsop	4,027

DIVISION THREE (SOUTH) NORTH CUP

Jan	5	(h)	Clapton O.	W	4-3	Hancocks, Kelly, Talbot, Alsop	4,000
	12	(h)	Port Vale	W	3-1	Alsop, Kelly, Hancocks	5,000
	19	(a)	Port Vale	L	0-1		4,000
	26	(h)	Mansfield T.	D	2-2	Hancocks 2	4,152
Feb	2	(a)	Mansfield T.	W	2-1	Kelly, Mullard	2,500
	9	(h)	Notts County	W	2-0	Hancocks, Wilshaw	5,144
	16	(a)	Notts County	L	0-1		12,116
	23	(a)	Clapton O.	W	1-0	Kelly	10,096
Mar	9	(a)	Southend Utd	D	2-2	Hancocks, Alsop	6,000
	16	(h)	Southend Utd	W	2-0	Alsop, Hancocks	8,228
	23	(a)	Aldershot	D	1-1	Talbot	3,547
	30	(h)	Aldershot	W	3-1	Talbot, Hancocks 2	9,232
Apr	6	(h)	Norwich City	W	4-2	Talbot, Hancocks, Mullard, Alsop	9,449
	13	(a)	Norwich City	D	1-1	Wilshaw	10,000
	20	(a)	Northampton T	W	4-1	Mullard 2, Talbot, Wilshaw	8,000
	22	(h)	Northampton T	W	3-1	Mullard 3	13,146
	27	(a)	Bristol R (SF)	W	3-1	Hancocks, Wilshaw, Talbot	14,673
May	4	(*)	Bournemouth (F)	L	0-1		19,715

* Played at Stamford Bridge, Chelsea F.C., and **Walsall fielded:-** Lewis; Methley, Shelton; Crutchley, Foulkes, Newman; Hancocks, Talbot, Mullard, Wilshaw, Alsop.

Appearances (League & Cup): J. Acquaroff 1, G. Alsop 32, H. Barratt 1*, W. Beckett 1*, G. Beech 3, S. Bennett 4, W.S. Brown 4, C.G. Bulger 5, G. Clark 3*, J. Clark 1, R. Crutchley 34, D. Darby 1*, A. Evans 4, J.L. Forder 1*, R.E. Foulkes 23, E. Gedders 1, W.C. Goffin 1, L. Hamers 1, J. Hancocks 27, E.J. Harding 2*, K. Harper 1, E. Harvey 1, S.E. Heaselgrave 2*, H.J. Hinks 1, G. Hinsley 1*, J. Jarvis 1, R.J. Jenkins 8, F.C. Kelly 16, J. Lewis 2*, John Lewis 31, H. Lowery 4*, N.A. Male 15, A. McNab 2*, I. Methley 17, A.T. Mullard 21, A.D. Newman 25, J. Paxton 1*, L.T. Payne 3, H.J. Peace 4, G. Pearce 1, W.T. Peck 2, R.T. Pritchard 1*, H. Rowlinson 1, J. Sankey 10*, J. Screen 7*, A. Shelley 2, J.B.T. Shelton 13, W. Skidmore 1*, E. Smith 1*, C. Stone 4, G.J. Strong 1, F.L. Talbot 24, E.J. Vinall 5*, R. Walker 2*, G. Walton 2, F.R.H. White 1*, B.F. Williams 3, D.J. Wilshaw 8*, T. Wood 1* — **Total 396.** * *Guest player.*

Goalscorers (L & C): Hancocks 14, Alsop 12, Kelly 12, Mullard 9, Talbot 7, Bennett 4, Wilshaw 4, Darby 3, Barratt 1, Bulger 1, Evans 1, Foulkes 1, Goffin 1, Jenkins 1, Vinall 1 — **Total 72.**

RECORD

	P	W	D	L	F	A	Pts	Post
FL (S-N)	20	6	3	11	31	42	15	9th
F.A. Cup	2	1	0	1	4	6		
Div 3 SN Cup	18	11	4	3	37	20		
Total	40	18	7	15	72	68		

TOP TEN WARTIME APPEARANCES

J.B.T. Shelton	191
N.A. Male	182
B.F. Williams	115
W.S. Brown	114
L.D. Morgan	111
T. Wood	109
G. Alsop	103
E.J. Vinall	101
J. Hancocks	92
J. Lewis	92

TOP TEN WARTIME GOALSCORERS

G. Alsop	58
E.J. Vinall	54
W.S. Brown	49
J. Hancocks	34
J.F. Rowley	23
T. Wood	20
J.H. Beesley	15
G. Hinsley	14
F.C. Kelly	12
R. Starling	12

Walsall's complete Wartime Record

Season	P	W	D	L	F	A
1939-40	35	10	7	18	64	91
1940-41	34	15	7	12	104	90
1941-42	31	13	1	17	63	79
1942-43	34	9	7	18	55	66
1943-44	35	8	13	14	44	66
1944-45	35	10	9	17	51	62
1945-46	40	18	7	15	72	68
7 seasons	245	83	51	111	453	522

Dennis Wilshaw

Sammy Heaselgrave

Jack Sankey

West Bromwich Albion

Season 1939-40

FOOTBALL LEAGUE DIVISION 2

Aug	26	(a)	Swansea	W	2-1	H. Jones 2	15,000
	28	(a)	Coventry	D	3-3	E. Jones, Banks, Connelly	26,000
Sept	2	(h)	Tottenham H	L	3-4	E. Jones 3	17,008

MIDLANDS REGIONAL LEAGUE

Oct	21	(h)	Luton T	W	3-1	Banks 2, Johnson	5,424
	28	(a)	Coventry C	L	3-6	Banks, H. Jones, Witcomb	3,056
Nov	4	(a)	Northampton T	D	1-1	H. Jones	4,643
	11	(h)	Leicester C	W	1-0	H. Jones	4,265
	18	(h)	Birmingham	D	2-2	H. Jones, Sankey (pen)	8,671
	25	(h)	Wolves	W	5-0	H. Jones 2, Bell, Newsome, Johnson	5,722
Dec	2	(a)	Walsall	W	2-0	H. Jones, Newsome	4,815
	9	(a)	Luton T	W	5-4	H. Jones 3, Newsome, Sankey (pen)	4,000
	16	(h)	Coventry C	W	3-1	H. Jones 2, Johnson	3,802
	23	(h)	Northampton T	W	4-1	H. Jones 2, Newsome, Bell	4,129
	26	(h)	Birmingham	W	3-0	H. Jones, Johnson, Sankey (pen)	6,934
	30	(a)	Leicester C	W	5-2	H. Jones (pen), Connelly, Johnson, Witcomb, Newsome	1,939
Jan	13	(a)	Wolves	L	0-2		9,412
	20	(h)	Walsall	W	7-2	H. Jones 3 (1 pen) Bell 2, Johnson 2	1,831
Feb	24	(h)	Birmingham	W	6-1	H. Jones 2, Newsome, Connelly, Johnson, Bell	6,799
Mar	2	(h)	Wolves	D	1-1	Johnson	8,641
	9	(a)	Walsall	D	1-1	Connelly	3,012
	16	(a)	Luton T	W	6-3	H. Jones 3, Newsome, Heaselgrave, Connelly	3,224
	23	(h)	Coventry C	W	3-1	Sankey 2, Connelly	6,743
	25	(h)	Birmingham	W	4-1	H. Jones 3, Newsome (pen)	9,986
	26	(h)	Leicester C	W	5-1	H. Jones 2, Newsome 2 (1 pen), Connelly	6,088
	30	(h)	Northampton T	W	4-1	H. Jones 2, Heaselgrave, Butler	5,504
Apr	6	(a)	Leicester C	L	2-5	H. Jones, Heaselgrave	5,006
	13	(h)	Luton T	W	3-1	H. Jones 3	3,398
Mar	13	(a)	Wolves	L	4-5	H. Jones, Newsome 2 (1 pen), Springthorpe (og)	6,014
	14	(h)	Walsall	L	2-3	Connelly, Newsome	1,567
June	5	(h)	Northampton T	W	2-1	Newsome, Heaselgrave	1,374
	8	(a)	Coventry C	L	0-4		3,998

LEAGUE CUP

Apr	20	(h)	Portsmouth	W	3-1	Connelly 2, Heaselgrave	11,511
	27	(a)	Portsmouth	L	2-3	H. Jones, Summerbee (og)	9,873
May	4	(a)	Bournemouth	W	2-1	H. Jones 2	9,665
	11	(h)	Bournemouth	W	3-1	H. Jones, Heaselgrave, Connelly	7,619
	18	(a)	Coventry C	W	1-0	(a.e.t) Sankey	8,901
	25	(a)	Blackburn R	L	1-2	Richardson	9,742

Albion's goalkeeper, Jimmy Adams.

Appearances (League & Cup): J. Adams 8, G.E. Banks 7, I.C.H. Bassett 11, T. Bell 15, S. Butler 3, G. Chapman 1, I. Clarke 4, E. Connelly 33, C. Davies 3, C.I. Edwards 1, W.B. Elliott 1, W.E. Gripton 29, Heaselgrave 17, J.A. Johnson 33, E.N. Jones 6, H.J. Jones 34, H. Kinsell 3, H. Lowery 5, A. McNab 33, R. Newsome 30, W.G. Richardson 2, J. Sankey 34, W. Saunders 29, C.E. Shaw 37, H. White 24, D.F. Witcomb 4 – **Total 407.**

Goalscorers (L & C): H. Jones 42, Newsome 14, Connelly 11, Johnson 9, Heaselgrave 6, Sankey 6, Bell 5, Banks 4, E. Jones 4, Witcomb 2, opponents 2, Butler 1, Richardson 1 – **Total 107.**

RECORD

P	W	D	L	F	A
37	23	5	9	107	67

West Bromwich Albion

Season 1940-41

FOOTBALL LEAGUE (SOUTH)

Aug	31	(h)	Walsall	W	3-1	Price 2, Heaselgrave	2,966
Sep	7	(a)	Walsall	W	2-0	Heaselgrave, Johnson	2,968
	14	(h)	Northampton T	W	4-1	Richardson 2, Newsome 2 (1 pen)	2,607
	21	(a)	Northampton T	D	1-1	Newsome (pen)	3,200
	28	(h)	Birmingham	L	1-2	Richardson	4,718
Oct	5	(a)	Birmingham	W	3-1	Newsome, Clarke, Johnson	5,394
	12	(h)	Stoke City	L	0-1		4,091
	19	(a)	Stoke City	W	3-1	Richardson 2, Johnson	3,392
	26	(h)	Notts County	W	3-1	Richardson 2, Hodgetts	2,496
Nov	2	(h)	Notts County	L	2-3	Sankey 2 (1 pen)	2,100
	9	(h)	Coventry C	L	1-4	Sankey (pen)	978
	23	(h)	Mansfield T	W	4-2	Richardson 2, Heaselgrave, Sankey (pen)	831
	30	(a)	Mansfield T	D	3-3	Richardson 2, Elliott	2,000
Dec	7	(h)	Nottingham F	W	5-0	Richardson 3, Heaselgrave, Elliott	1,261
	14	(a)	Leicester C	L	3-4	Heaselgrave 2, Richardson	939
	21	(h)	Leicester C	L	4-5	Richardson 3, Elliott	765
	28	(h)	Nottingham F	W	5-3	Richardson 2, Elliott 2, Heaselgrave	1,839
Mar	15	(h)	Stoke City	D	2-2	Richardson, Sankey	2,086
	22	(a)	Stoke City	W	2-0	Elliott 2	794
	29	(h)	Walsall	W	4-1	H. Jones 2, Elliott, Richardson	1,412
Apr	5	(a)	Walsall	D	3-3	Wilkes 2, Heaselgrave	1,850
	12	(a)	Northampton T	L	1-3	Elliott	2,141
	19	(h)	Northampton T	W	3-2	Chapman, Sankey, Hunter (og)	1,463
May	3	(a)	Reading	L	3-6	Heaselgrave, Richardson, Wilkes	4,000
	17	(a)	Cardiff C	D	4-4	Elliott 2, Wilkes, C. Evans	3,009
	31	(a)	Walsall	L	3-10	Johnson, Elliott, Sankey	1,512

MIDLAND CUP

Jan	11	(h)	Notts County	W	8-1	Elliott 2, Heaselgrave 2, Richardson 2, Chapman, Johnson	1,403
Feb	8	(a)	Walsall	L	3-4	Johnson 2, Elliott	3,135

LEAGUE CUP

Feb	15	(a)	Notts County	L	0-4		2,700
	22	(h)	Notts County	W	5-0	Heaselgrave 2, Richardson 2, C. Shaw (pen)	2,581
Mar	1	(h)	Mansfield T	L	2-3	Richardson 2	2,132
	8	(a)	Mansfield T	L	2-6	Gripton 2	2,800

Appearances (League & Cup): J. Adams 30, J. Alderwick 1, I.C.H. Bassett 19, G. Chapman 12, I. Clarke 9, E. Connelly 14, C. Davies 1, G. Dudley 6, C.I. Edwards 24, W.B. Elliott 19, C.J. Evans 2, E.I. Goodall 1*, W.E. Gripton 28, S.E. Heaselgrave 26, F. Hodgetts 2, J.A. Johnson 24, E.N. Jones 2, H.J. Jones 4, T.H. Kinsell 24, H. Lowery 6, A McNab 5, R. Newsome 9, W. Price 1*, W. Quinton 1*, W.G. Richardson 26, J. Sankey 30, C.E. Shaw 20, G.A. Wilkes 3, D.F. Witcomb 3 — Total 352. * *Guest player.*

Goalscorers (L & C): Richardson 29, Elliott 15, Heaselgrave 13, Johnson 7, Sankey 7, Newsome 4, Wilkes 4, Chapman 2, Gripton 2, H. Jones 2, Price 2, Clarke 1, Evans 1, Hodgetts 1, Shaw 1, opponent 1 — **Total 92.**

RECORD

P	W	D	L	F	A
32	14	5	13	92	82

Season 1941-42

FOOTBALL LEAGUE (SOUTH)

Aug	30	(h)	Cardiff City	W	6-3	H. Jones 4, Elliott, Johnson	4,462
Sep	6	(a)	Cardiff City	D	1-1	C. Edwards	4,647
	13	(h)	Leicester C	W	4-1	C. Evans 2, Richardson, Johnson	3,786
	20	(a)	Leicester C	L	2-3	Elliott, Sankey	3,526
	27	(a)	Walsall	L	1-2	Elliott	4,494
Oct	4	(h)	Walsall	W	4-0	Elliott, Heaselgrave, Wilkes, Evans	4,135
	11	(a)	Aston Villa	W	3-2	H. Jones, Elliott 2	5,500
	18	(h)	Swansea T	W	8-0	Richardson 5, Elliott 2, Evans	537
Nov	8	(a)	Wolves	W	8-2	Elliott 3, Evans 3, Johnson, Sankey	6,000
	15	(h)	Wolves	W	5-3	Elliott 2, Richardson 2, Dudley	3,774
	22	(h)	Luton T	W	10-1	Richardson 6, Evans 2, Elliott, Johnson	2,618
	29	(a)	Luton T	W	5-4	Richardson 2, Elliott 2, Clarke	2,200
Dec	6	(h)	Northampton T	W	7-0	McKennan 3, Elliott 2, Richardson, Sankey	1,766
May	23	(h)	Walsall	W	3-1	Bowen, Elliott, Ashley	1,695

WARTIME LEAGUE CUP

Dec	27	(h)	Wrexham	W	6-4	Richardson 2, Elliott 2, McKennan, Evans	4,497
Jan	3	(a)	Wrexham	D	5-5	Richardson 2, McKennan, Dearson, Elliott	2,500
	10	(h)	Stoke	W	4-0	Richardson, Elliott, McKennan, Johnson	7,335
	17	(a)	Stoke	L	1-2	Elliott	4,578
Feb	14	(h)	Leicester C	W	3-2	Richardson 2, Elliott	4,378
	21	(h)	Mansfield T	W	3-1	McKennan 2, Richardson	1,398
Mar	7	(a)	Northampton T	L	3-4	Elliott 2, Evans	2,000
	14	(h)	Northampton T	D	2-2	McKennan, Johnson	3,706
	21	(a)	Leicester C	L	2-4	Sankey, Gripton	5,685
Apr	4	(a)	Stoke City	L	3-5	Johnson, Elliott, Evans	5,000
	6	(h)	Stoke City	W	6-1	Richardson 2, McKennan 2 (1 pen), Elliott, Sankey	13,400
	11	(a)	Cardiff City	D	1-1	Richardson	10,781
	18	(h)	Cardiff City	W	3-2	Richardson 2, Elliott	10,198
	25	(h)	Everton	W	3-1	Evans, Elliott, Edwards	19,006
May	2	(a)	Everton	W	5-1	Elliott 2, McKennan 2, Evans	34,000
	9	(h)	Wolves	L	0-4		35,000
	16	(a)	Wolves	L	0-3		29,000

Appearances (League & Cup): J. Adams 25, H. Ashley 3*, G. Banks 1, I. Bassett 29, T.H. Bowen 1, I. Clarke 4, D.J. Dearson 1*, G. Dudley 6, C.I. Edwards 27, W.B. Elliott 31, C.J. Evans 31, W.E. Gripton 26, W. Harris 2, S.E. Heaselgrave 9, J.A. Johnson 20, C.W. Jones 1, H.J. Jones 3, T.H. Kinsell 1, H. Lowery 1, P. McKennan 15*, A McNab 15, G.C. May 1, G.H. Merrick 3*, W. Quinton 1*, W.G. Richardson 24, J. Sankey 25, C.E. Shaw 30, G.A. Wilkes 1, J.G. Willetts 1, D.F. Witcomb 3 — **Total 341.** * *Guest player.*

Goalscorers (L & C): Elliott 31, Richardson 31, Evans 14, McKennan 13, Johnson 7, Sankey 5, H. Jones 4, Edwards 2, Ashley 1, Bowen 1, Clarke 1, Dearson 1, Dudley 1, Gripton 1, Heaselgrave 1, Wilkes 1 — **Total 115.**

RECORD

P	W	D	L	F	A
31	18	4	9	115	69

West Bromwich Albion

Cliff Edwards

'Sandy' McNab

Doug Witcomb

Season 1942-43

FOOTBALL LEAGUE NORTH (1st COMPETITION)

Aug	29	(a)	Northampton T	L	0-2		4,882
Sep	5	(h)	Northampton T	L	6-3	Elliott 3, Sankey 2, Evans	1,500
	12	(h)	Leicester C	W	3-2	Millard 3	4,000
	19	(a)	Leicester C	D	0-0		4,029
	26	(a)	Wolves	L	0-2		8,382
Oct	3	(h)	Wolves	W	6-2	Millard 3, Elliott 2, Evans	7,813
	10	(h)	Aston Villa	W	6-2	Elliott 2, Shaw, Millard, Evans, Finch	10,326
	17	(a)	Aston Villa	L	2-8	Heaselgrave 2	12,000
	24	(a)	Derby C	L	0-4		7,810
	31	(h)	Derby C	D	3-3	Heaselgrave 2, Newsome (pen)	4,571
Nov	7	(h)	Stoke City	D	0-0		4,564
	14	(a)	Stoke City	L	1-5	Clarke	3,331
	21	(h)	Walsall	D	0-0		2,783
	28	(a)	Walsall	L	0-2		3,412
Dec	5	(n)	Birmingham	L	0-3		3,000
	12	(h)	Birmingham	W	4-3	Ashley 2, Sankey, Dudley	3,393
	19	(a)	Coventry C	L	1-2	Ashley	5,000
	25	(h)	Coventry C	W	3-0	Ashley 2, Witcomb	5,199
Apr	3	(n)	Birmingham	L	3-5	Richardson 3	4,000
	10	(h)	Birmingham	L	0-4		1,818
	17	(h)	Walsall	W	4-0	Richardson 2, Jones, A. Evans	1,575
	24	(a)	Walsall	W	2-1	Richardson, Finch	1,500
	26	(h)	Northampton T	W	6-1	Richardson 3, Clarke 2, A. Evans	2,468
May	1	(a)	Aston Villa	W	6-2	Richardson 5, Jones	5,613

FOOTBALL LEAGUE NORTH (2nd COMPETITION)

Dec	26	(h)	Leicester C	W	5-1	Elliott 3 (1 pen), Hodgetts, Dudley	8,119
Jan	2	(a)	Leicester C	L	0-9		3,578
	9	(h)	Coventry C	L	2-3	Elliott (pen), Sankey	3,676
	16	(a)	Coventry C	L	0-1		8,500
	23	(a)	Aston Villa	W	5-3	Doherty 2, Green Elliott, Evans	12,000
	30	(h)	Aston Villa	W	2-1	Elliott (pen), Shaw	13,200
Feb	6	(n)	Birmingham	W	1-0	Green	8,000
	13	(h)	Birmingham	W	2-1	Elliott (pen), Jones	7,217
	20	(a)	Wolves	L	0-1		12,444
	27	(h)	Wolves	W	2-0	Evans, Shaw	10,138
Mar	6	(a)	Coventry C	D	1-1	Evans	11,502
	13	(h)	Coventry C	W	3-0	Lane, Dearson, Elliott	13,332
	20	(h)	Chesterfield	L	2-3	Elliott 2	13,447
	27	(a)	Chesterfield	D	3-3	Richardson 3	13,661

Appearances (League & Cup): J. Adams 33, H. Ashley 9*, I.C.H. Bassett 19, G. Billingsley 1*, A. Brown 1*, M. Burgin 2, H. Butler 1, K. Butler 1, S. Butler 2, J.H. Bye 1*, G. Chapman 1, I Clarke 5, A. Davenport 1, C. Davies 4, D.J. Dearson 4*, P. Doherty 2*, G. Dudley 6, M. Dunkley 1*, C. Edwards 3, W.B. Elliott 24, A.J. Evans 6, C.J. Evans 36, L.C. Finch 19, T. Green 3*, W.E. Gripton 29, E.A. Hapgood 3*, W. Harris 1, S.E. Heaselgrave 12, F. Hodgetts 13, J.A. Johnson 2, E.N. Jones 3, H.J. Jones 2, S. Jones 1*, T.H. Kinsell 1, H. Lane 2*, J.C. McDonald 6, A. McNab 17, G. Marks 1*, L. Millard 35, R. Newsome 4, A. Parker 2, W.G. Richardson 14, E. Robinson 1, J. Sankey 26, L. Scott 2*, C. Shaw 11, J.B.T. Shelton 5*, H. Simms 1, T. Smalley 1*, A.J. Smith 30*, J. Smith 2*, W. Walsh 1*, D.F. Witcomb 4, T. Wood 1* — **Total 418.** * *Guest player.*

Goalscorers (L & C): Elliott 17, Richardson 17, Millard 7, C. Evans 6, Ashley 5, Heaselgrave 4, Sankey 4, Clarke 3, Shaw 3, Doherty 2, Dudley 2, A. Evans 2, Finch 2, Green 2, E. Jones 2, Dearson 1, Hodgetts 1, H. Jones 1, Lane 1, Newsome 1, Witcomb 1 — **Total 84.**

RECORD

P	W	D	L	F	A
38	17	6	15	84	83

West Bromwich Albion

Season 1943-44

FOOTBALL LEAGUE (NORTH) FIRST COMPETITION

Aug	28	(h)	Derby County	W	3-2	Richardson, Evans, Armstrong	5,926
Sep	4	(a)	Derby County	W	5-1	Richardson 4, Jones	6,393
	11	(h)	Northampton T	D	4-4	Elliott 4 (1 pen)	6,222
	18	(a)	Northampton T	L	1-2	Elliott	3,721
	25	(h)	Wolves	W	4-1	Richardson 2, Elliott, Duns	7,363
Oct	2	(a)	Wolves	W	3-2	Richardson 2, Duns	8,819
	9	(a)	Leicester C	W	3-0	Richardson 2, Hodgetts	6,971
	16	(h)	Leicester C	D	2-2	Richardson 2	7,090
	23	(a)	Aston Villa	L	1-3	Richardson	19,000
	30	(h)	Aston Villa	W	5-4	Richardson 2, Elliott 2, Evans	23,550
Nov	6	(a)	Stoke City	D	3-3	Richardson, Elliott (pen), Hodgetts	3,520
	13	(h)	Stoke City	W	3-0	Richardson 2, C. Evans	6,912
	20	(a)	Walsall	L	0-2		4,297
	27	(h)	Walsall	L	1-4	Duns	4,556
Dec	4	(h)	Birmingham	L	1-3	Elliott	5,494
	11	(a)	Birmingham	L	0-3		5,156
	18	(h)	Coventry C	W	3-0	Elliott 2, Clarke	2,647
	25	(a)	Coventry C	L	0-8		7,000

FOOTBALL LEAGUE NORTH (SECOND COMPETITION)

Dec	27	(h)	Birmingham	D	1-1	Elliott (pen)	14,717
Jan	1	(a)	Birmingham	L	0-4		9,142
	8	(a)	Walsall	D	2-2	Ball 2	5,793
	15	(h)	Walsall	W	7-1	Ball 3, Elliott 3, Witcomb	4,800
	22	(h)	Coventry C	D	2-2	Elliott, Witcomb	5,577
	29	(a)	Coventry C	D	3-3	Elliott 2, Ball	8,500
Feb	5	(a)	Northampton T	L	0-2		4,381
	12	(h)	Northampton T	W	3-1	Ball 2, Hodgetts	4,503
	19	(h)	Stoke City	L	2-8	Duns, Elliott	5,000
	26	(a)	Stoke City	L	4-5	Elliott 3, Duns	8,030
Apr	10	(a)	Aston Villa	L	1-4	Heaselgrave	15,000

MIDLAND CUP MATCHES

Mar	4	(h)	Nottingham F	L	0-1		3,392
	11	(a)	Nottingham F	L	2-3	Pears, Russell	6,346
	18	(h)	Wolves	W	5-0	Elliott 3, Hodgetts, Guest	4,588
	25	(a)	Wolves	D	3-3	Heaselgrave 2, Guest	6,281
Apr	1	(a)	Walsall	D	2-2	Acquaroff 2	2,120
	8	(h)	Walsall	W	1-0	Acquaroff	5,588
	15	(a)	Stoke City	D	1-1	Elliott	3,434
	22	(h)	Stoke City	W	3-1	Elliott, Heaselgrave, Richardson	7,202
	29	(h)	Nottingham F	D	2-2	Richardson, Evans	8,373
May	6	(a)	Nottingham F	W	4-3	Acquaroff 2, Hodgetts, Clarke (a.e.t)	14,438

Appearances (League & Cup): J. Acquaroff 5*, J. Adams 10, J.B. Adderley 1, M. Armstrong 8*, H. Ashley 1*, H.G. Ball 10, I.C.H. Bassett 14, D.J. Bradley 1, I. Clarke 4, L. Duns 13*, C.I. Edwards 4, W.B. Elliott 26, A.J. Evans 4, C.J. Evans 33, L.C. Finch 5, J. Griffiths 1*, W.E. Gripton 38, W.F. Guest 4*, S.E. Heaselgrave 11, N.H. Heath 29, F. Hodgetts 24, E.N. Jones 7, J. McCormick 6*, A. McNab 27, L. Millard 39, W.G. Pears 1, J.T. Pemberton 1, W.G. Richardson 19, G.A. Rowley 1, T.J. Russell 4, J. Sankey 6, A.J. Smith 32*, J.H. Southam 23, H. White 2, G.H. Wilcoxson 1, G. Williams 6, D.F. Witcomb 8 — **Total 429.** * *Guest player.*

Goalscorers (L & C): Elliott 28, Richardson 21, Ball 8, Acquaroff 5, Duns 5, Hodgetts 5, C. Evans 4, Heaselgrave 4, Clarke 2, Guest 2, Witcomb 2, Armstrong 1, E. Jones 1, Pears 1, Russell 1 — **Total 90.**

RECORD

P	W	D	L	F	A
39	14	11	14	90	93

Len Millard

Harry 'Popeye' Jones

West Bromwich Albion

Season 1944-45

FOOTBALL LEAGUE (NORTH) FIRST CHAMPIONSHIP

Aug	26	(a)	Northampton T	W	4-1	Evans, Richardson, Elliott (pen), Hodgetts	5,890
Sep	2	(h)	Northampton T	W	3-1	Heaselgrave 2, Hodgetts	5,998
	9	(h)	Port Vale	W	2-1	Rowley, Elliott	7,749
	16	(a)	Port Vale	D	0-0		6,000
	23	(a)	Coventry C	D	1-1	Clarke	8,245
	30	(h)	Coventry C	W	4-1	Clarke 3, Hodgetts	9,512
Oct	7	(h)	Leicester C	D	1-1	Heaselgrave	9,970
	14	(a)	Leicester C	W	2-0	Evans, Clarke	7,201
	21	(a)	Aston Villa	D	2-2	Rowley (pen), Clarke	25,200
	28	(h)	Aston Villa	L	1-5	Clarke	25,487
Nov	4	(h)	Stoke City	L	2-3	Elliott, Evans	18,656
	11	(a)	Stoke city	W	3-2	Clarke 3	8,067
	18	(a)	Wolves	L	2-3	Clarke, Johnson	12,485
	25	(h)	Wolves	W	3-2	Heaselgrave, Evans, Elliott	5,916
Dec	2	(h)	Walsall	W	3-0	Elliott 2, Clarke	8,992
	9	(a)	Walsall	W	2-1	Clarke 2	5,303
	16	(a)	Birmingham	L	0-2		6,796
	23	(h)	Birmimgham	L	1-4	Heaselgrave	5,000
	26	(a)	Aston Villa	W	4-3	Clarke 3, McNab	5,007

FOOTBALL LEAGUE NORTH

Apr	2	(h)	Aston Villa	L	2-4	Heaselgrave, Evans	14,378
	7	(h)	Walsall	D	1-1	Clarke	5,227
	14	(a)	Walsall	W	2-1	Clarke, Bowen	1,780
May	5	(a)	Birmingham	L	1-4	Clarke	1,025
	12	(h)	Birmingham	L	2-3	Saunders, Evans	10,947
	19	(a)	Wolves	L	0-1		6,702
	26	(h)	Wolves	D	1-1	Hodgetts	4,742

FOOTBALL LEAGUE SECOND COMPETITION

Dec	30	(h)	Coventry C	D	1-1	Heaselgrave	8,659
Jan	6	(h)	Aston Villa	L	1-3	Ball	21,995
	13	(a)	Aston Villa	L	2-6	McNab, Heaselgrave	15,000
Feb	3	(h)	Walsall	L	0-2		6,334
	10	(a)	Walsall	D	0-0		6,376
	17	(h)	Birmingham	W	4-0	Clarke 3, Smith	12,479
	24	(a)	Birmingham	D	1-1	Heaselgrave	17,727
Mar	3	(a)	Coventry C	W	3-0	Hodgetts 2, Smith	7,048
	10	(a)	Northampton T	D	2-2	Heaselgrave 2	6,200
	17	(h)	Northampton T	W	6-0	Clarke 3, Heaselgrave, Johnson, Coley (og)	6,938
	24	(a)	Bristol City	L	2-5	Clarke, Elliott	21,371
	31	(h)	Bristol City	D	3-3	Parker, Heaselgrave, Clarke	18,315

MIDLAND CUP

Apr	21	(h)	Leicester C	W	1-0	Clarke	5,002
	28	(a)	Leicester C	L	0-3		6,166

Note: Match on 26th December v Aston Villa (a) was abanonded after 81 minutes due to fog but the result was allowed to stand.

Appearances (League & Cup): J. Adams 5, H.G. Ball 6, R.J. Barlow 1, T.H. Bowen 5, I. Clarke 35, G. Dudley 1, W.B. Elliott 13, C.J. Evans 23, R. Finch 6, W.E. Gripton 39, G.F.M. Hardwick 3*, S.E. Heaselgrave 35, N.H. Heath 6, F. Hodgetts 40, J.A. Johnson 9, E.N. Jones 4, T.H. Kinsell 7, E. Lewis 28, H. Lowery 15, A. McNab 37, N.A. Male 1*, L. Millard 38, A. Parker 3, H. Parkes 6*, W.G. Richardson 4, G.A. Rowley 6, J. Sankey 9, D.G. Saunders 3*, W. Saunders 1, J.B.T. Shelton 1*, L.G.F. Smith 3*, J.H. Southam 9, G.H. Tranter 16, E.A. Vincent 1, G. Williams 21 — **Total 440.** * *Guest player.*

Goalscorers (L & C): Clarke 29, Heaselgrave 13, Elliott 7, Evans 6, Hodgetts 6, Johnson 2, McNab 2, Rowley 2, Smith 2, Ball 1, Bowen 1, Parker 1, Richardson 1, D. Saunders 1, opponent 1 — **Total 75.**

RECORD

P	W	D	L	F	A
40	15	11	14	75	74

Joe Johnson

Billy Gripton

West Bromwich Albion

Season 1945-46

FOOTBALL LEAGUE (SOUTH)

Aug	25	(h)	Swansea T.	W	4-1	Clarke, Barlow, Millard, Hodgetts	18,033
	29	(h)	Aston Villa	W	1-0	Millard	15,898
Sep	1	(a)	Swansea T	W	4-2	Barlow 2, Hodgetts, White (pen)	8,223
	5	(a)	Aston Villa	D	3-3	Elliott (pen), Clarke, Saunders	36,103
	8	(a)	Birmingham	L	0-4		20,068
	12	(h)	Luton T	W	3-1	Clarke, Elliott, Barlow	14,146
	15	(h)	Birmingham	D	0-0		27,745
	22	(h)	Tottenham H	W	5-0	Barlow 3, Pears, Butler	26,002
	29	(a)	Tottenham H	L	2-4	Barlow, Ward (og)	31,403
Oct	6	(h)	Brentford	L	3-4	Rowley 2, Barlow	29,821
	13	(a)	Brentford	L	0-2		20,160
	20	(a)	Chelsea	L	4-7	Hodgetts, Elliott, Barlow, Butler	31,061
	27	(h)	Chelsea	W	8-1	Clarke 4, Rowley 2, Hodgetts, Witcomb	21,905
Nov	3	(h)	Millwall	W	3-1	Clarke, Rowley, Hodgetts	16,046
	10	(a)	Millwall	W	4-1	Clarke, Rowley, Barlow, Hodgetts	20,045
	17	(a)	Southampton	W	2-1	Elliott, Clarke	17,116
	24	(h)	Southampton	W	5-2	Elliott 3, Hodgetts, Rowley	18,768
Dec	1	(h)	Derby County	L	2-3	Elliott, Rowley	29,525
	8	(a)	Derby County	D	3-3	Newsome 2, Barlow	24,138
	15	(a)	Leicester C	W	3-1	Elliott, Newsome, Millard	14,227
	22	(h)	Leicester C	W	3-2	Elliott 2, Newsome	15,107
	24	(h)	Coventry C	D	2-2	Clarke, Newsome	18,038
	26	(a)	Coventry C	L	2-3	Clarke, Newsome	19,303
	29	(a)	Luton T	W	2-1	Connelly, Saunders	9,146
Jan	12	(a)	Arsenal	L	0-2		22,334
	19	(h)	Arsenal	L	0-1		26,014
Feb	2	(a)	Charlton A.	D	1-1	Clarke	25,083
	9	(a)	Fulham	W	4-1	Elliott, Newsome 2, Freeman (og)	15,139
	16	(h)	Fulham	W	3-1	Elliott 2, Butler	20,229
	23	(h)	Plymouth A	W	5-2	Clarke 2, Elliott, Connelly, Gomm	13,117
Mar	2	(a)	Plymouth A	W	4-0	Newsome 2, Connelly, Butler	20,227
	9	(a)	Portsmouth	L	0-3		15,987
	16	(h)	Portsmouth	W	2-0	Elliott, Jinks	15,908
	23	(h)	Nottingham F	W	1-0	Banks	19,755
	30	(a)	Nottingham F	W	2-0	Butler, Hodgetts	21,529
Apr	6	(a)	Newport C	W	3-0	Clarke, Banks, Butler	14,014
	13	(h)	Newport C	W	6-0	Clarke 3, Hodgetts, Butler Millard	18,690
	15	(h)	Charlton A	L	2-5	Banks, Elliott	5,187
	20	(a)	West Ham U	D	1-1	Elliott	24,630
	22	(a)	Wolves	D	0-0		36,361
	23	(h)	Wolves	D	1-1	Banks	38,077
	27	(h)	West Ham U	L	1-2	Elliott (pen)	11,821

Jim Sanders

Cecil Shaw

F.A. CUP

Jan	5	(a)	Cardiff C	R3/1	1-1	Connelly	28,928
	9	(h)	Cardiff C	R3/2	4-0	Clarke 2, Newsome 2	18,025
	26	(a)	Derby Co.	R4/1	0-1		31,440
	30	(h)	Derby Co.	R4/2	1-3	Clarke	35,882

Appearances (League): G.E. Banks 8, R.J. Barlow 32, D.J. Bradley 1, S. Butler 25, I. Clarke 35, E. Connelly 10, C.I. Edwards 1, W.B. Elliott 34, C.J. Evans 4, B. Gomm 4, W.E. Gripton 6, W. Harris 12, S.E. Heaselgrave 1, F. Hodgetts 29, G.O. Hood 1, J. Jinks 1*, T.H. Kinsell 31, L. Millard 37, R. Newsome 12, W. Pears 3, G.A. Rowley 9, R.A. Ryan 17, J.A. Sanders 27, D.G. Saunders 2, W. Saunders 2, C.E. Shaw 29, J.H. Southam 2, G.H. Tranter 34, W.L. Twigg 1, H. White 13, G. Williams 1, N. Williams 1, D.F. Witcomb 37 — **Total 462.** ** Guest player.*

Goalscorers (L & C): Clarke 19, Elliott 19, Barlow 12, Newsome 10, Hodgetts 9, Rowley 8, Butler 7, Banks 4, Millard 4, Connelly 3, D. Saunders 2, Gomm 1, Jinks 1, Pears 1, White 1, Witcomb 1, opponents 2 — **Total 104.**

F.A. Cup Appearances: S. Butler 2, I. Clarke 4, E. Connelly 4, W.B. Elliott 4, F. Hodgetts 1, H.F. Kinsell 4, L. Millard 4, R. Newsome 4, J.A. Sanders 3, D.G. Saunders 1, C.E. Shaw 4, G.H. Tranter 4, W.L. Twigg 1, D.F. Witcomb 4 — **Total 44.**

F.A. Cup Goalscorers: Clarke 3, Newsome 2, Connelly 1 — **Total 6.**

RECORD

F.L. South	42	22	8	12	104	69
F.A. Cup	4	1	1	2	6	5
Totals	46	23	9	14	110	74

TOP TEN WARTIME APPEARANCES

W. Gripton	194
L. Millard	153
W. Elliott	152
A. McNab	133
J. Sankey	132
C.E. Shaw	130
C.J. Evans	129
S.E. Heaselgrave	111
J. Adams	110
F. Hodgetts	109

TOP TEN WARTIME GOALSCORERS

W. Elliott	117
W.G. Richardson	100
I. Clarke	58
H.J. Jones	49
S.E. Heaselgrave	41
C.J. Evans	31
R. Newsome	31
J.A. Johnson	25
D. Hodgetts	22
J. Sankey	22

Albion's complete Wartime Record

Season	**P**	**W**	**D**	**L**	**F**	**A**
1939-40	37	23	5	9	107	67
1940-41	32	14	5	13	92	82
1941-42	31	18	4	9	115	69
1942-43	38	17	6	15	84	83
1943-44	39	14	11	14	90	93
1944-45	40	15	11	14	75	74
1945-46	46	23	9	14	110	74
7 Seasons	263	124	51	88	673	542

Frank Hodgetts

Reg Ryan

Wolves

Season 1939-40

FOOTBALL LEAGUE DIVISION 1

Aug	26	(h)	Arsenal	D	2-2	Dorsett, Westcott	41,222
	29	(a)	Grimsby T.	D	0-0		8,129
Sep	2	(a)	Blackpool	L	1-2	McAloon	22,036

Appearances: S. Cullis 3, R. Dorsett 3, T. Galley 3, J. Gardiner 3, J. Maguire 3, G. McAloon 1, A. McIntosh 2, W. Morris 3, J. Mullen 3, R.A. Scott 3, F. Taylor 3, D. Westcott 3 — Total 33.

Goalscorers: Dorsett 1, McAloon 1, Westcott 1 — **Total 3.**

MIDLAND REGIONAL LEAGUE

Oct	21	(a)	Birmingham	L	2-3	Dorsett, Westcott	6,428
	28	(h)	Northampton	W	7-2	Westcott 4, McMahon 2, W. Wright	3,500
Nov	4	(h)	Walsall	W	4-1	McMahon, F. Taylor, Westcott, W. Wright	4,517
	11	(a)	Luton Town	D	2-2	Mullen, Westcott	8,000
	18	(h)	Coventry C.	W	4-0	Westcott 2, Mullen, Frith (og)	5,210
	25	(a)	W.B.A.	L	0-5		5,722
Dec	2	(h)	Leicester C.	W	5-0	Westcott 3, Dorsett, King	5,147
	9	(h)	Birmingham	W	6-2	Westcott 3 Dorsett 2, Mullen	2,705
	16	(a)	Northampton	W	2-1	Dorsett, Westcott	6,657
	23	(a)	Walsall	W	5-3	Dorsett 4, Westcott	5,448
	30	(h)	Luton Town	W	4-1	Dorsett 2, Westcott 2	2,996
Jan	6	(a)	Coventry C.	W	3-0	Westcott 2, Dorsett	1,879
	13	(h)	W.B.A.	W	2-0	Dorsett 2	9,412
	20	(a)	Leicester C.	W	2-1	Dorsett, McIntosh	1,800
Feb	24	(h)	Coventry C.	W	1-0	McMahon	2,532
Mar	2	(a)	W.B.A.	D	1-1	McMahon	8,641
	9	(h)	Leicester C.	W	5-1	McMahon 3, McIntosh, Mullen	2,446
	16	(h)	Birmingham	W	3-1	Galley, McIntosh, McMahon	4,351
	23	(a)	Northampton	L	0-2		5,870
	30	(a)	Walsall	W	2-1	Galley, W. Wright	6,106
Apr	6	(h)	Luton Town	W	6-1	Westcott 3, Galley Mullen, H. Wright	2,943
	10	(a)	Birmingham	W	1-0	Westcott	7,227
	13	(a)	Coventry C.	D	1-1	W. Wright	3,046
May	1	(a)	Luton Town	L	0-3		4,034
	13	(h)	W.B.A.	W	5-4	W. Taylor 4, Mullen	6,014
	18	(h)	Walsall	L	1-5	Gardiner	5,038
	25	(a)	Leicester C.	L	1-3	Somerfield	3,340
June	1	(h)	Northampton	W	1-0	Mullen	2,016

LEAGUE CUP

Apr	20	(a)	Wrexham	R1/1	1-1	Westcott	9,752
	27	(h)	Wrexham	R1/2	3-0	Dorsett 3	5,471
May	4	(h)	Coventry C.	R2/1	0-2		6,035
	11	(a)	Coventry C.	R2/2	2-5	W. Wright 2	8,713

Appearances (Regional League & Cup): J. Alderton 2, A. Bainbridge 1, H. Brown 1, T. Burnden 3, J. Buttery 1, S. Clewlow 2, S. Cullis 3, R. Dorsett 16, J. Dowen 7*, L. Finch 1*, T. Galley 26, J. Gardiner 24, L. Glasberg 1, R. Goddard 29, F. King 2, A. McIntosh 23, D. McMahon 6, J. Mullen 32, W. Parker 5, F. Pedley 2, S. Puckett 1, R.A. Smith 6, C. Sidlow 26, T. Smalley 3*, A.J. Smith 2, A Somerfield 1, T. Springthorpe 10, A. Steen 23, F. Taylor 27, W. Taylor 2, D. Thornhill 22, D. Westcott 21, H. Wright 1, W. Wright 20 — Total 352. * *Guest player.*

Goalscorers (L & C): Westcott 27, Dorsett 19, McMahon 9, Mullen 7, W. Wright 6, W. Taylor 4, Galley 3, McIntosh 3, W. Wright 3, Gardiner, King, McAloon, Somerfield, F. Taylor, H. Wright, opponent, one goal each — **Total 85.**

RECORD

P	W	D	L	F	A
35	20	6	9	85	56

*Wolves did not field a team in any competition during season 1940-41.

Alex Mcintosh

Tom Smalley

Frank Taylor

Wolves

Season 1941-42

FOOTBALL LEAGUE (SOUTH)

Aug	30	(a)	Bristol City	L	2-4	Wright, Alderton	5,964
Sep	6	(h)	Bristol City	L	1-2	Mullen	6,892
	27	(a)	Leicester City	L	0-2		3,850
Oct	4	(h)	Leicester City	D	0-0		4,121
	11	(h)	Cardif City	L	0-3		2,935
	18	(a)	Cardiff City	L	0-2		2,494
	25	(h)	Walsall	W	1-0	Galley	3,527
Nov	1	(a)	Walsall	L	1-4	Gardiner	2,408
	8	(h)	W.B.A.	L	2-8	Ashton, McIntosh	6,005
	15	(a)	W.B.A.	L	3-5	Westcott 2, McIntosh	3,774
	22	(a)	Northampton	W	2-1	Westcott 2	2,939
	29	(h)	Northampton	W	2-1	Mullen 2	5,114
Dec	6	(a)	Nottm Forest	D	0-0		1,414
	13	(h)	Nottm Forest	W	7-0	Westcott 6, Wright	4,035
	20	(a)	Walsall	W	2-1	O'Donnell 2	1,529
	25	(h)	Walsall	W	4-3	Wright 2, Dorsett, Galley	3,895

LEAGUE CUP QUALIFYING COMPETITION

Dec	27	(h)	Chester	W	2-1	Stevenson, Wright	5,053
Jan	3	(a)	Chester	W	3-1	Curtis, Stevenson, Mullen	3,498
	10	(a)	Blackpool	L	1-6	Mullen	6,026
	17	(h)	Blackpool	W	1-0	Wright	4,972
	31	(a)	Everton	L	1-2	Mullen	9,116
Feb	7	(a)	Wrexham	W	3-0	Stevenson, Wright, Westcott	1,438
	14	(h)	Wrexham	W	4-1	Mullen 2, Stevenson 2	4,109
	21	(h)	Manchester C.	L	1-3	Westcott	5,878
	28	(a)	Manchester C.	L	1-4	Dorsett	4,885
Mar	7	(h)	Everton	W	11-1	Rowley 5, Broome 3, Westcott 2, Stevenson	4,932

LEAGUE CUP PROPER

Apr	4	(h)	Chester	R1/1	3-1	Westcott 2, Mullen	7,273
	6	(a)	Chester	R1/2	1-0	Wescott	2,854
	11	(a)	Man. Utd.	R2/1	4-5	Westcott 3, Brown	9,227
	18	(h)	Man. Utd.	R2/2	2-0*	Dorsett, Westcott	12,341
	25	(h)	Man. City	R3/1	2-0	Westcott 2	15,071
May	2	(a)	Man. City	R3/2	0-1		14,715
	9	(a)	W.B.A.	SF/1	4-1	Robinson 2, Westcott, Broome	35,036
	16	(h)	W.B.A.	SF/2	3-0	Mullen, Westcott, Robinson	29,030
	23	(a)	Sunderland	F/1	2-2	Westcott 2	34,776
	30	(h)	Sunderland	F/2	4-1	Rowley 2, Westcott, Broome	43,038

* After extra time

CHALLENGE MATCH v. LONDON CUP WINNERS

June	6	(n)	Brentford	D	1-1	Mullen	20,174

(Played at Stamford Bridge)

Appearances (League & Cup): J. Alderton 15, T. Asbridge 1, D. Ashton 29, W. Aston 1, H. Barrett 1, F. Broome 8*, H. Brown 2, W. Brown 1, C. Burton 1, R. Christopher 1, G. Clarke 9, W. Crook 1, S. Cullis 1, G. Curtis 2, F. Davenport 6, R. Dorsett 16, J. Dowen 22*, J. Dunningham 1, T. Galley 10, J. Gardiner 8, R. Goddard 8, A. Goldthorpe 1, M. Hambly 1, D. Johnstone 1*, R. Kirkham 1, J. Leitch 1*, R. Marsh 1*, J. McCormack 4*, J. McDonald 1*, A. McIntosh 4, T. McIntosh 3, R. Morgan 2*, J. Mullen 28, F. O'Donnell 4*, R. Pritchard 1, E. Robinson 5, J. Rowley 2*, R.A. Scott 9, W. Shorthouse 1, C. Sidlow 18, B. Singleton 9, A.J. Smith 3, T. Springthorpe 24, E. Stevenson 29, F. Taylor 14, T. Taylor 1, D. Thornhill 35, L. Turner 3, C. Trigg 1, D. Walker 4, J. Wardle 1, D. Westcott 20, H. Wright 1, W. Wright 28 — **Total 407**. * *Guest player.*

Goalscorers: Westcott 28, Mullen 11, Rowley 7, W. Wright 7, Stevenson 6, Broome 5, Dorsett 3, Robinson 3, Galley 2, McIntosh 2, O'Donnell 2, Alderton, Ashton, Brown, Curtis, Gardiner all one each — **Total 81**.

RECORD

P	W	D	L	F	A
37	19	4	14	81	66

Roy Pritchard

Bill Shorthouse

Terry Springthorpe

Wolves

Season 1942-43

FOOTBALL LEAGUE NORTH (1st COMPETITION)

Aug	29	(a)	Aston Villa	L	0-2		14,884
Sep	5	(h)	Aston Villa	L	1-2	Westcott	8,047
	12	(h)	Stoke City	W	3-2	Westcott 3	4,251
	19	(a)	Stoke City	L	0-1		5,029
	26	(h)	W.B.A.	W	2-0	Westcott 2	8,382
Oct	3	(a)	W.B.A.	L	2-6	Westcott 2	7,813
	10	(h)	Walsall	W	3-2	Stevenson, Westcott, Shelton (og)	6,105
	17	(a)	Walsall	L	2-5	Pritchard, Westcott	4,990
	24	(a)	Crewe Alex.	L	1-4	Westcott	3,489
	31	(h)	Crewe Alex.	W	3-2	Clarke, Gardiner, Crook	2,968
Nov	7	(a)	Coventry C.	L	0-1		10,257
	14	(h)	Coventry C.	D	1-1	Dunn	4,904
	21	(h)	Derby County	W	8-1	Rowley 8	3,128
	28	(a)	Derby County	L	1-3	Barrass	9,223
Dec	5	(h)	Leicester City	L	0-2		1,954
	12	(a)	Leicester City	L	0-5		5,139
	19	(h)	Birmingham	D	1-1	Barrass	1,198
	25	(a)	Birmingham	L	0-1		2,029

FOOTBALL LEAGUE (NORTH) SECOND CHAMPIONSHIP

Dec	26	(a)	Aston Villa	L	0-1		20,074
Jan	2	(h)	Aston Villa	L	0-4		5,838
	9	(h)	Wrexham	W	4-0	Westcott 3, Dorsett	4,175
	16	(a)	Wrexham	D	3-3	Westcott 2, Pritchard	4,190
	23	(h)	Stoke City	D	4-4	Wright 3, Pritchard	6,226
	30	(a)	Stoke City	D	2-2	Wright, McIntosh	5,847
Feb	6	(a)	Crewe Alex.	W	3-0	Rowley, Stevenson, Galley	4,554
	13	(h)	Crewe Alex.	W	6-1	Wright 3, Dorsett, Rowley 2	4,106
	20	(h)	W.B.A.	W	1-0	Dorsett	12,444
	27	(a)	W.B.A.	L	0-2		10,138
Mar	20	(a)	Wrexham	L	1-3	Crowe	2,467
Apr	17	(a)	Crewe Alex.	L	1-8	Gardiner	2,583
	24	(a)	Stoke City	W	4-1	Dorsett 2, Westcott 2	2,677
	26	(a)	Tranmere R.	L	1-3	Walters	1,206
May	1	(a)	Derby Co.	D	3-3	Ball, Galley, McLean	5,258

* Matches played from 26th December to 27th February inclusive were also League Cup qualifying games.

LEAGUE CUP (NORTH) COMPETITION PROPER

(These matches also counted in League (North) Second Championship)

Mar	6	(a)	Aston Villa	R1/1	2-5	Bailey, Dorsett	25,145
	13	(h)	Aston Villa	R1/2	3-5	Dorsett 2, Dunn	15,109

Appearances (League & Cup): J. Alderton 18, D. Ashton 30, G. Attenborough 1, A. Bailey 1*, S. Ball 3, M. Barrass 3, C. Battiste 1, D. Bilton 3, H. Bowden 1*, C. Buchanan 7, T. Burden 2, G. Clark 5, A. Crook 1, W. Crook 19, V. Crowe 4, S. Cullis 5, D. Darby 3, R. Dorsett 7, J. Dowen 22*, J. Dunn 24, D. Emanuel 1*, J. Ford 2, N. Franklin 1*, T. Galley 14, J. Gardiner 16, J. Greenaway 1, J. Hooks 1*, J. Jackman 10, L. Kelly 7, R. King 1, R. Kirkham 2, A. McIntosh 4, A. McClean 28, I. Methley 2*, R. Michael 1, J. Morby 1, W. Morgan 1, J. Mullen 4, A. Mulraney 4*, L. Mynard 1, J. O'Neill 1, J. Pleasant 1, J. Pringle 1, R. Pritchard 12, T. Reece 1*, G. Reeves 2, D. Roberts 9, J. Rowley 1, G.A. Rowley 8*, W. Shorthouse 1, C. Sidlow 31, B. Singleton 1, W. Skidmore 2, A. Somerfield 1, T. Springthorpe 1, A. Steen 1, A. Stephens 2, E. Stevenson 3, F. Taylor 2, D. Thornhill 9, D. Walker 1, H. Walters 4, D. Westcott 13, H. Wright 2, W. Wright 10 — **Total 385.** * *Guest player.*

Goalscorers (L & C): Westcott 18, J. Rowley 8, Dorsett 8, W. Wright 7, Pritchard 3, G. A. Rowley 3, Barrass 2, Dunn 2, Galley 2, Gardiner 2, Stevenson 2, Bailey, Ball, Clarke, Crook, Crowe, McIntosh, McLean, Walters, opponent, all one goal each — **Total — 66.**

RECORD

P	W	D	L	F	A
35	10	6	19	66	86

Dennis Westcott

Billy Wright

Wolves

Season 1943-44

FOOTBALL LEAGUE (NORTH) FIRST COMPETITION

Aug	28	(h)	Crewe Alex.	L	2-4	Lee, Dorsett	4,808
Sep	4	(a)	Crewe Alex.	W	2-1	Aldecoa, McLean	5,207
	11	(h)	Aston Villa	L	2-4	Dunn, Aldecoa	10,045
	18	(a)	Aston Villa	L	1-4	Isherwood	14,499
	25	(a)	W.B.A.	L	1-4	Crook	8,117
Oct	2	(h)	W.B.A.	L	2-3	Crook, Wilshaw	10,083
	9	(a)	Stoke City	L	0-5		5,119
	16	(h)	Stoke City	L	1-2	Isherwood	7,245
	23	(a)	Walsall	W	3-1	Lee 2, Westcott	3,794
	30	(h)	Walsall	D	1-1	Westcott	11,829
Nov	6	(h)	Coventry C.	W	2-1	Aldecoa 2	4,006
	13	(a)	Coventry C.	D	1-1	Bicknell	7,168
	20	(h)	Derby County	L	1-3	Aldecoa	6,037
	27	(a)	Derby County	D	2-2	Stephens, McLean	6,845
Dec	4	(a)	Leicester C.	L	0-1		5,223
	11	(h)	Leicester C.	W	4-1	Stephens 2, McLean, Dunn	3,869
	18	(a)	Birmingham	L	2-4	Aldecoa 2	4,030
	25	(h)	Birmingham	W	3-0	Lee, Aldecoa, Rowley	7,177

FOOTBALL LEAGUE (NORTH) SECOND CHAMPIONSHIP

Dec	26	(h)	Stoke City	D	1-1	Aldecoa	6,240
Jan	1	(a)	Stoke City	L	3-9	Jackman, Wright, Westcott	6,798
	8	(a)	Coventry C.	L	2-3	Westcott 2	6,356
	15	(h)	Coventry C.	D	2-2	Stephens, Dunn	7,856
	22	(h)	Aston Villa	L	0-4		12,313
	29	(a)	Aston Villa	L	1-3	Davies	16,031
Feb	5	(h)	Birmingham	L	0-2		7,044
	12	(a)	Birmingham	L	1-2	Dowen	7,778
	19	(a)	Walsall	D	0-0		2,188
	26	(h)	Walsall	D	1-1	Wilshaw	3,885
Mar	4	(h)	Northampton T.	L	1-4	McLean	3,492
	11	(a)	Northampton T.	L	2-7	McLean, Davies	3,556
	18	(a)	W.B.A.	L	0-5		4,588
	25	(h)	W.B.A.	D	3-3	Wilshaw, Davies, Dowen	6,281
Apr	1	(h)	Wrexham	L	0-1		5,118
	10	(h)	Leicester C.	W	4-1	McLean 2, Mullen 2	9,941
1 5		(a)	Chester	W	3-1	Buchanan 2, Davies	3,880
	22	(h)	Chester	L	0-4		8,028
	29	(a)	Stoke City	D	2-2	Wilshaw, Aldecoa	2,156
May	6	(h)	Stoke City	W	2-1	McLean, Aldecoa	1,997

* Matches played from 26th December to 26 February inclusive also counted as League Cup qualifying games. Wolves failed to qualify for competition proper.

Appearances (League & Cup): E. Aldecoa 32, J. Alderton 11, D. Ashton 30, A. Atkins 1, R. Bicknell 3, G. Billingsley 6*, D. Bilton 3, M. Buckby 1, G. Clark 1, G. Crilly 1, A. Crook 8, W. Crook 33, V. Crowe 5, S. Cullis 2, K. Davies 10, R. Dorsett 6, J. Dowen 4*, J. Dunn 25, T. Galley 7, J. Gardiner 2, F. Haycock 7*, L. Hayward 2, D. Hazelton 1, R. Houghton 1*, D. Isherwood 2, J. Jackman 2, L. Kelly 22, R. Kirkham 13, K. Lee 9, W. Lovesey 1, K. Malcolm 1, A. McLean 37, W. Morgan 3, J. Mullen 2, J. Mulvaney 1*, I. Owen 4, S. Pickstock 2, H. Prince 10, R. Pritchard 8, D. Roberts 1, J. Rowley 3*, J. Shelton 1*, W. Shorthouse 1, W. Skidmore 6, C. Sidlow 14, A. Stephens 24, B. Streton 4*, F. Taylor 3, D. Thornhill 2, W. Wagg 1, J. Wallis 1, H. Walters 10, D. Westcott 5, D. Wilshaw 11, T. Wood 2*, H. Wright 1, W. Wright 3 — **Total 418**. * *Guest player.*

Goalscorers (L & C): Aldercoa 11, McLean 8, Westcott 5, Davies 4, Lee 4, Stephens 4, Wilshaw 4, Dunn 3, Buchanan 2, Crook 2, Dowen 2, Isherwood 2, Mullen 2, Bicknell, Dorsett, Jackman, Rowley, W. Wright all one each — **Total 58**.

RECORD

P	W	D	L	F	A
38	8	9	21	58	98

Dicky Dorsett

Cyril Sidlow

Angus McLean

Wolves

Season 1944-45

FOOTBALL LEAGUE (NORTH) FIRST CHAMPIONSHIP

Aug	26	(a)	Leicester City	D	2-2	Haycock, Dorsett	10,175
Sep	2	(h)	Leicester City	W	4-0	Acquaroff 2, Aldecoa, Finch	7,948
	9	(h)	Aston Villa	L	1-2	Acquaroff	14,124
	16	(a)	Aston Villa	L	1-3	Acquaroff	20,069
	23	(a)	Stoke City	L	0-2		13,806
	30	(h)	Stoke City	W	4-1	Alderton, H. Wright, Finch, Acquaroff	12,134
Oct	7	(h)	Northampton T.	D	2-2	W. Wright, Acquaroff	10,240
	14	(a)	Northampton T.	D	1-1	Dorsett	3,523
	21	(h)	Walsall	D	1-1	Acquaroff	9,697
	28	(a)	Walsall	W	2-1	W. Wright, Acquaroff	7,225
Nov	4	(a)	Birmingham	L	0-1		12,073
	11	(h)	Birmingham	L	0-4		8,008
	18	(h)	W.B.A.	W	3-2	Acquaroff 2, Crook	12,485
	25	(a)	W.B.A.	L	2-3	Dunn, Finch	5,916
Dec	2	(a)	Port Vale	W	3-0	Davies, Acquaroff, Dunn	5,884
	9	(h)	Port Vale	W	2-0	Aldecoa, Dunn	8,038
	16	(h)	Coventry C.	D	1-1	Davies	6,148
	23	(a)	Coventry C.	W	2-1	Davies, Acquaroff	5,044

FOOTBALL LEAGUE (NORTH) SECOND CHAMPIONSHIP

Dec	26	(h)	Walsall	D	1-1	Kirkham	7,759
	30	(a)	Stoke City	L	0-2		9,896
Jan	6	(a)	Crewe Alex.	W	3-2	Acquaroff 2, Davies	3,496
	13	(h)	Crewe Alex.	W	3-1	Mitten, W. Wright, Acquaroff	7,010
	20	(h)	Chester	W	6-1	Jinks 3, Dunn, Aldecoa 2	5,192
Feb	3	(a)	Port Vale	L	0-2		4,839
	10	(h)	Port Vale	L	1-2	Rowley	6,886
	17	(h)	Wrexham	W	4-1	Acquaroff 3, Wharton	10,143
	24	(a)	Wrexham	D	1-1	Dunn	8,746
Mar	3	(h)	Stoke City	L	1-3	Buchanan	17,784
	10	(h)	Leicester City	W	3-2	Fenton 2, Williams	7,856
	17	(a)	Chester	W	4-0	Fenton, Dunn, King, Johnson	4,047
Apr	2	(h)	Birmingham	W	2-1	Mullen, Wilshaw	12,031
May	19	(h)	W.B.A.	W	1-0	King	6,702
	21	(a)	Aston Villa	D	4-4	Wright 2, Smith, Potts	6,994
	26	(a)	W.B.A.	D	1-1	W. Wright	4,472

* Matches from 30th December to 17th March inclusive also counted as League Cup qualifying games.

WARTIME GUESTS

Mick Fenton (Middlesbrough)

Laurie Scott (Arsenal)

LEAGUE CUP (NORTH) COMPETITION PROPER

Mar	24	(a)	Aston Villa	R1/1	2-1	W. Wright, Alderton	29,953
	31	(h)	Aston Villa	R1/2	1-0	Mullen	39,333
Apr	7	(a)	Birmingham	R2/1	0-0		30,184
	14	(h)	Birmingham	R2/2	1-0*	Morris	30,066
	21	(h)	Cardiff City	R3/1	3-0	W. Wright 2, Kirkham	34,927
	28	(a)	Cardiff City	R3/2	1-2	Finch	40,283
May	5	(h)	Bolton Wds.	SF/1	2-2	Dunn, Mullen	28,149
	12	(a)	Bolton Wds.	SF/2	1-2	Heathcote	29,682

* This game was after extra-time, Morris scoring the winning goal in the 153rd minute of the match.

Matches in this competition also counted as League (North) Second Championship fixtures. And the match v. Birmingham on 14th April was 0-0 at full-time and recorded as a draw in the League Championship.

Bill Morris

Billy Crook

Jimmy Dunn

Appearances (League & Cup): J. Acquaroff 24*, E. Aldecoa 16, J. Alderton 35, D. Ashton 33, S. Ball 1, R. Bennett 1, R. Bicknell 2, A.R. Brown 1*, C. Buchanan 7, W. Crook 37, V. Crowe 1, K. Davies 19, R. Dorsett 6, J. Dowen 4*, J. Dunn 28, M. Fenton 2*, L. Finch 31*, J. Harris 6, R. Harris 1, F. Haycock 1*, W. Heathcote 2*, W. Green 1, H. Iddon 1*, J. Jackman 1, J. Jinks 1*, W. Johnson 2*, D. Jones 1*, L. Kelly 2, M. Kelly 1, F. King 1, J. Kirkham 16*, K. Lee 4, G. McAloon 1, A. McLean 25, C. Mitten 1*, W. Morris 32, J. Mullen 6, L. Mynard 2, D. Parsons 1, G. Paterson 1*, J. Paxton 2, V. Potts 1, R. Pritchard 1, D. Roberts 5, J. Rowley 1*, L. Scott 2*, R.A. Scott 39, W. Skidmore 1, C. Sidlow 2, A.J. Smith 8*, L.J. Smith 3, A. Somerfield 3, A. Stephens 2, D. Westcott 1, G. Wharton 4*, G. Williams 1, D. Wilshaw 2, H. Wright 2, W. Wright 21 — **Total 462**. * *Guest player.*

Goalscorers (L & C): Acquaroff 18, W. Wright 9, Dunn 7, Finch 5, Davies 4, Aldecoa 3, Fenton 3, Jinks 3, Mullen 3, Alderton 2, Dorsett 2, Kirkham 2, Buchanan, Crook, Haycock, Heathcote, Johnson, King, Lee, Mitten, Morris, Potts, Rowley, L. Smith, Wharton, Williams, Wilshaw, H. Wright and one each — **Total 77**.

P	W	D	L	F	A
42	18	12	12	77	58

Wolves

Season 1945-46

FOOTBALL LEAGUE (SOUTH)

Aug	25	(a)	Tottenham H.	W	4-1	Bennett, Smith Wright, Chatham	33,852
	27	(h)	Charlton Ath.	L	1-2	Smith	25,142
Sep	1	(h)	Tottenham H.	W	4-2	King 2, Smith, Chatham	24,674
	3	(h)	Arsenal	D	1-1	Dunn	25,360
	8	(h)	Brentford	W	1-0	Chatham	19,895
	15	(a)	Brentford	D	0-0		20,664
	22	(a)	Chelsea	D	1-1	Wright	34,918
	29	(h)	Chelsea	W	1-0	Darby	29,679
Oct	6	(h)	Millwall	L	1-2	Darby	30,118
	13	(a)	Millwall	L	0-2		29,745
	20	(a)	Southampton	W	4-2	Buchanan 3, Darby	20,058
	27	(h)	Southampton	W	3-2	Mullen 2, Dorsett	21,837
Nov	3	(h)	Derby Co.	W	1-0	Ramscar	25,140
	10	(a)	Derby Co.	L	0-2		22,204
	17	(a)	Leicester City	W	2-1	Chatham, Dunn	17,486
	24	(h)	Leicester City	W	3-0	Chatham 2, Mullen	22,099
Dec	1	(h)	Coventry City	W	1-0	Dunn	19,730
	8	(a)	Coventry City	L	0-1		13,824
	15	(a)	Luton Town	L	0-1		9,896
	20	(h)	Luton Town	W	3-0	King, Westcott, Chatham	18,155
	25	(h)	Aston Villa	L	1-2	Mullen	30,071
	26	(a)	Aston Villa	D	1-1	Wright	59,970
	29	(a)	Arsenal	L	2-3	Galley, Wright	37,970
Jan	12	(a)	Fulham	L	1-3	Chatham	34,009
	19	(h)	Fulham	W	2-0	Miller, Davies	18,022
Feb	2	(a)	Plymouth Arg.	L	2-3	Chatham 2	10,134
	9	(a)	Portsmouth	W	2-0	Crook, Wright	17,246
	16	(h)	Portsmouth	W	4-0	Chatham 3, Wright	20,006
	23	(h)	Nottm Forest	W	4-0	Wright 3, Chatham	20,349
Mar	2	(a)	Nottm Forest	D	0-0		22,150
	9	(a)	Newport Co.	W	3-1	Davies, Crook, opponent o.g.	15,676
	16	(h)	Newport Co.	W	5-2	Westcott 3, Dorsett 2	26,233
	23	(a)	Swansea Town	W	5-2	Westcott, King, Dorsett 2, McIntosh	25,935
	30	(h)	Swansea Town	W	1-0	Dorsett	25,042
Apr	6	(h)	West Ham U.	D	3-3	King, Westcott, Dorsett	24,526
	13	(a)	West Ham U.	L	1-2	Westcott	25,028
	20	(h)	Birmingham	D	3-3	Westcott 3	42,684
	22	(h)	W.B.A.	D	0-0		36,361
	23	(a)	W.B.A.	D	1-1	Westcott	38,077
	27	(a)	Birmingham	W	1-0	opponent o.g.	24,991
	29	(h)	Plymouth Arg.	D	1-1	Westcott	16,734
May	4	(a)	Charlton Ath.	D	1-1	Dorsett	47,035

League Appearances: J. Alderton 31, D. Ashton 23, R. Bennett 6, R. Bicknell 2, C. Buchanan 2, R. Chatham 29, W. Crook 31, S. Cullis 13, K. Davis 11, D. Darby 6, R. Dorsett 7, J. Dunn 23, T. Galley 15, C. Gibson 2*, R. Goddard 4, W. Green 2, J. Harris 1, J. Jackman 1, F. King 25, R. Kirkham 3, J. Maguire 1, I. Methley 1, A. McIntosh 9, A. McLean 34, D. Miller 11, W. Morris 31, J. Mullen 12, J. Paxton 8, R. Pritchard 1, F. Ramscar 10, J. Rowley 1*, J. Sanderson 1, R.A. Scott 10, C. Sidlow 3, L.J. Smith 10, A. Steen 5, A. Stephens 4, D. Westcott 13, B. Williams 29, W. Wright 31 — **Total 462.** * *Guest player.*

League goalscorers: Chatham 14, Westcott 12, Wright 9, Dorsett 8, King 5, Mullen 4, Buchanan 3, Darby 3, Dunn 3, Smith 3, Crook 2, Davies 2, Bennett, Galley, McIntosh, Miller, Ramscar all one each, opps. 2 — **Total 75.**

F.A. CUP

Jan	5	(a)	Lovells Ath.	R3/1	4-2	Davies 2, Galley, Crook	10,057
	9	(h)	Lovells Ath.	R3/2	8-1	Galley 3, Dunn, Wright 2, King, Mullen	14,885
	26	(a)	Charlton A.	R4/1	2-5	Chatham 2	44,271
	30	(h)	Charlton A.	R4/2	1-1	Wright	27,720

* This competition was the first and only time the competition has been run on a two-legged basis up to and including the quarter-finals.

F.A. Cup appearances: J. Alderton 4, D. Ashton 4, R. Bicknell 1, R. Chatham 2, W. Crook 4, S. Cullis 1, K. Davies 2, J. Dunn 4, T. Galley 2, L. Kelly 1, R. King 4, A. McLean 2, W. Morris 3, J. Mullen 2, B. Williams 4, W. Wright 4 — **Total 44.**

Goalscorers: Galley 4, Wright 3, Chatham 2, Davies 2, Crook 1, Dunn 1, King 1, Mullen 1 — **Total 15.**

RECORD

	P	W	D	L	F	A	Pts
League (s)	42	20	11	11	75	48	51
F.A.C.	4	2	1	1	15	9	—
Total	46	22	12	12	90	57	—

David Miller
11 appearances

Ray Chatham
leading scorer in 1945-46

TOP TEN WARTIME APPEARANCES

D. Ashton	149
A. McLean	126
W. Crook	125
W. Wright	117
J. Alderton	116
J. Dunn	104
C. Sidlow	94
J. Mullen	89
T. Galley	77
D. Westcott	76

TOP TEN WARTIME GOALSCORERS

D. Westcott	91
R. Dorsett	42
W. Wright	34
J. Mullen	28
J. Acquaroff	18
J. Rowley	17
R. Chatham	16
J. Dunn	16
E. Aldecoa	14
T. Galley	12

Wolves's complete Wartime Record

Season	P	W	D	L	F	A
1939-40	35	20	6	9	85	56
1940-41	Did not enter any competition					
1941-42	37	19	4	14	81	66
1942-43	35	10	6	19	66	86
1943-44	38	8	9	21	58	98
1944-45	42	18	12	12	77	58
1945-46 (L)	42	20	11	11	55	48
1945-46	4	2	1	1	15	9
Totals	233	97	49	87	457	421